Taunton's COMPLETE ILLUSTRATED *Guide to*

Turning

RICHARD RAFFAN

The Taunton Press

Text © 2005 by Richard Raffan
Photographs © 2005 by The Taunton Press, Inc., except p. 29 (bottom right photo) by Terry Golbeck
Illustrations © 2005 by The Taunton Press, Inc.

The Taunton Press
Inspiration for hands-on living®

The Taunton Press, Inc., 63 South Main Street, PO Box 5506, Newtown, CT 06470-5506
e-mail: tp@taunton.com

EDITOR: Paul Anthony
DESIGN: Lori Wendin
LAYOUT: Cathy Cassidy
ILLUSTRATOR: Mario Ferro
PHOTOGRAPHER: Richard Raffan

LIBRARY OF CONGRESS CATALOGING-IN-PUBLICATION DATA:
Raffan, Richard.
 Taunton's complete illustrated guide to turning / Richard Raffan.
    p. cm.
ISBN: 978-1-56158-672-1 hardcover
ISBN: 978-1-62710-765-5 paperback
 1. Turning. 2. Lathes. I. Title.
 TT201.R33 2004
 684'.08--dc22
                        2004012690

Printed in the United States of America
10 9 8 7 6 5 4 3 2 1

The following manufacturers/names appearing in *Taunton's Complete Illustrated Guide to Turning* are trademarks: Dremel®, Tormek®, U-Beaut Enterprises®, WD-40®

About Your Safety: Working with wood is inherently dangerous. Using hand or power tools improperly or ignoring safety practices can lead to permanent injury or even death. Don't try to perform operations you learn about here (or elsewhere) unless you're certain they are safe for you. If something about an operation doesn't feel right, don't do it. Look for another way. We want you to enjoy the craft, so please keep safety foremost in your mind whenever you're in the shop.

Acknowledgments

Bringing together a book like this is never a solo effort, and I'm most grateful for the help and comments offered by many fellow turners.

Thanks to Mike Scott, Robin Wood, and David Woodward in England and Wales for allowing me to photograph them in action in their workshops.

Nearer home, thanks to my brother Simon and his slabbing skills, and to Gordon Smith, Peter Filmer, and Peter Bloomfield for access to their woodpiles and tools.

Thanks to both Graeme Bensley at Carbatec Tools, Fyshwick, my local woodturning store, and Terry Golbeck of Black Forest Wood Co., Calgary, where I teach occasionally, for all manner of bits and pieces of information as well as photos.

To Les Fortescue, who has more tools than he needs and kindly lent me a few for the deep hollowing photos.

To Paul Anthony—who asked the right questions and made editing most enjoyable.

And thanks finally to my wife Liz, who coped stoically (mostly) with the long and anti-social hours writing and editing seemed to demand.

Contents

PART TWO Preparation · 36

PART THREE Spindle Work · 94

PART FOUR Turning End Grain · 120

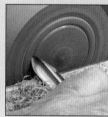

Introduction

THE WOOD LATHE IS ONE OF THE oldest means of mass production, along with the potter's wheel and metal casting. Round wooden objects so pervade our daily lives that we tend to forget that all those variations on spindles and knobs are turned. Most turnery is now mass produced on automatic copy lathes, but almost within living memory most was done by hand on man-powered machines.

In the 17th century, mechanically minded European aristocrats became the first hobby turners, working on lathes that cost more than most families earned in a year. And although small inexpensive hobby lathes were marketed through the great mail order catalogs of the early 20th century, it was not until the mid-1970s that woodturning started to become a popular retirement hobby.

Since the mid-1970s, interest in woodturning has increased exponentially and been transformed by a new breed of professional studio woodturner who creates one-off objects rather than mass producing just a few standard items. In the 21st century, lathe-based art is working its way into art galleries.

Much of the attraction of woodturning is the speed with which an object can be completed. Its very low establishment costs are also a factor, and the fact that raw material abounds often costing little more than your time to retrieve it. But a lathe only spins the wood. What is crafted from that spinning wood depends on the skill and vision of the individual at the lathe. This book can set you on the way to a new passion, and happy hours turning wood.

How to Use This Book

IRST OF ALL, this book is meant to be used, not put on a shelf to gather dust. It's meant to be pulled out and opened on your bench whenever you have a problem or want to try something new. So the first thing is to make sure this book is near where you do your woodworking and, particularly, woodturning.

In the pages that follow you'll find all the important processes and procedures for turning wood on a lathe. There's important advice on setting up the workspace and the preparation that is essential before you start turning.

Woodturning is a set of techniques that enable you to shape wood rapidly on a lathe. It is possible to get excellent results with a limited range of tools, and it's one of the least expensive areas of woodworking in which to get set up.

There are few variations on the basic techniques. The way gouges, chisels, and scrapers are used to cut and turn wood is much the same way all over the world. What separates the master, the apprentice, and the novice is practice and experience. All woodturners use the tools in much the same way to achieve much the same result, but practice and experience enable the masters to get there faster and circumvent problems before they arise. However, many novices create flawless work of the highest quality through determination and knowing what they want to achieve.

To find your way around the book, you first need to ask yourself three questions: What am I trying to make? Which sort of turning am I considering: face-work, center-work, or end-grain hollowing? What tools do I need to use to accomplish the task?

To organize the material, we've broken the subject down to two levels: "Parts" are major divisions of all aspects of woodturning; "Sections" contain related advice and techniques.

The first thing you'll see in a part is a group of photos keyed to a page number. Think of this as an illustrated table of contents. Here you'll see a photo representing each section of that part, along with the page on which each section starts.

Within sections, essential information and general advice is followed by basic techniques and procedures. Projects show how these combine as work proceeds.

Each section begins with a similar "visual map," with photos that represent the major groupings of information, procedures, and techniques. Under each grouping is a list of the step-by-step essays that explain how to go about particular jobs, and the pages on which they can be found.

Sections begin with an "overview," or brief introduction, to the information that follows. Here's where you'll find important general information on this group of techniques, including any safety issues. You'll read about specific tools and about ways of fixing wood on the lathe for the operations that follow.

The step-by-step essays are the heart of this book. Here a group of photos represents the key steps in the process or procedure. The accompanying text describes the process or best course of action and guides you through it, referring you back to the photos. Depending on

how you learn best, either read the text first or look at the photos; but remember, they are meant to work together. In cases where there is an alternative method, this is shown in a separate essay.

For efficiency, we've cross-referenced processes covered elsewhere or steps described in another similar procedure. You'll see yellow "cross-references" called out in the overviews and step-by-step essays.

When you see this symbol ⚠ make sure you read what follows. The importance of these safety warnings cannot be overemphasized. Always work safely and use safety devices. Never operate a machine without

The "VISUAL MAP" tells you where to locate the essay that details the operation you wish to do.

A "SECTION" groups related processes together.

The "OVERVIEW" gives you important general information about the group of techniques, tells you how to build jigs and fixtures, and provides advice on tooling and safety.

eye protection, and always wear a faceshield when turning anything other than a small short lightweight object between centers. It is a certain fact that wood spinning on a lathe will one day fly apart, and you must protect yourself against this reality at all times or risk injury. If you don't feel comfortable with a technique, lower the speed of the lathe and consider carefully what you have to do and how you should do it. If you are having a lot of catches, rotate the lathe by hand against the chisel or gouge, and work out what's happening in slow motion.

At the back of the book is an index to help you find what you're looking for in a pinch. There's also a list of further reading that will explain turning techniques in greater detail and give you insights into areas of health and safety, sharpening, converting timber, and shop layout.

Remember to use this book whenever you need to refresh your memory or to learn something new. It's been designed as an essential reference to help you become a better woodturner and woodworker. The only way it can do this is to make it as familiar a workshop tool as your favorite bowl gouge.

–The editors

"STEP-BY-STEP ESSAYS" contain photos, drawings, and instructions on how to do the technique.

"CROSS-REFERENCES" tell you where to find a related process or the detailed description of a process in another essay.

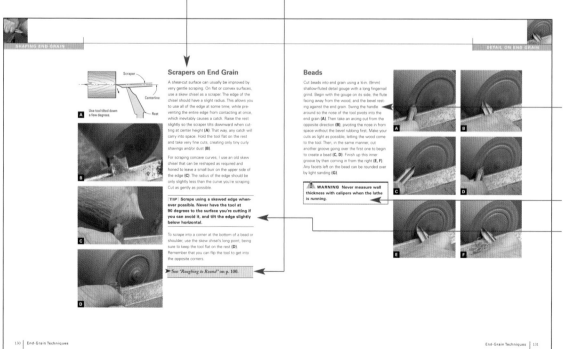

The "TEXT" contains keys to the photos and drawings.

"WARNINGS" tell you specific safety concerns for this process and how to address them.

"TIPS" show shortcuts and smart ways to work.

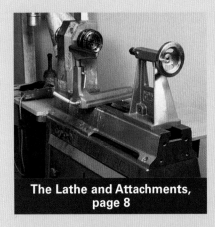

The Lathe and Attachments, page 8

Shaping Tools, page 15

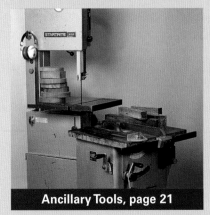

Ancillary Tools, page 21

Wood, page 28

PART ONE

Tools and Materials

WOODTURNING CAN BE DIVIDED broadly into center work (which is long and thin), end-grain projects (such as knobs and hollowed forms), and face work (which is wide and flattish).

Each discipline has its own set of tools, so it's tempting to rush out and purchase everything you might need someday. But if you want to avoid collecting stuff you'll never use, you'll do better to acquire tools and machines as you need them, and then get the best you can afford.

Eventually you might have several lathes, each for a different sort or scale of turning. The tools you acquire will depend on what you are making but will always include a grinder, some measuring and layout equipment, and probably a saw for cutting blanks. It's unlikely you'll ever have too many chucks, unless you turn only spindles.

In Part One, I discuss the array of lathes and tools available and try to help you sort out which equipment best suits your needs—which might be different from your "wants."

The Lathe
and Attachments

THE LATHE

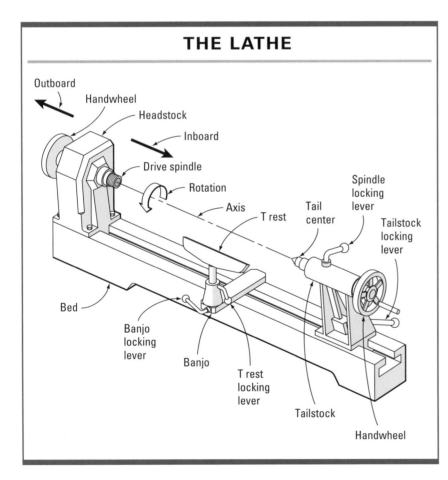

Outboard

Handwheel

Headstock

Inboard

Drive spindle

Rotation

Axis

T rest

Tail center

Spindle locking lever

Tailstock locking lever

Bed

Banjo locking lever

Banjo

T rest locking lever

Tailstock

Handwheel

A LATHE IS ESSENTIAL FOR WOOD-TURNING but, sadly, no one lathe is ideal for every aspect of the craft. When you go looking for—or set about constructing—a lathe, you need at least a vague idea of the type of work you want to turn. Otherwise, you'll be like the guy who purchases a family sedan to haul gravel when what he needs is a dump truck. The sedan will do the job, but it's not ideal. Only after you've decided on the sort of things you want to turn will you be able to assess which size and type of lathe you need.

Regardless of size, a standard lathe consists of a fixed headstock at the left end of the bed and a moveable tailstock to the right, which can be locked down at any point along the bed. A tail center is used when mounting center work and some face work. The drive center in the headstock and the tail center should be aligned exactly on the lathe axis. Between the headstock and tailstock is a tool rest, which supports the tool as cutting proceeds.

Power is usually transmitted from the motor to the drive shaft via a belt running on step pulleys. The lathe speed is varied by adjusting the belt on the pulleys. In recent years, electronic variable-speed controllers have become a very desirable but more expensive option. A variable-speed control allows you to adjust the speed instantly while the lathe is running, so it's worth having if you can afford it. Unfortunately, the controller boxes are large and awkward to locate when attached to benchtop models and small lathes, but that's a small price to pay for the convenience.

A standard lathe enables you to turn just about anything, so all you need is a lathe large enough for the jobs you have in mind. The lathe I use most of the time swings 23$\frac{5}{8}$ in. (600mm) while allowing 15$\frac{3}{4}$ in. (400mm) between centers. It is large and heavy enough for any bowl or vessel I'm likely to turn and will swing 88-lb. (40-kg) blanks. It's also a pleasure to use for small production items, but there is not enough distance between the centers for standard balusters or newel posts. I could purchase another section of bed and increase the center-work capacity, but I sold my long-bed Vicmarc, identical to the one shown at center right, and now use a smaller lathe that occupies less space.

For spindles up to 3 in. (75mm) in diameter and 32 in. (810mm) long, I use a small lathe with an extension bed. It has a long tool rest to make life easier.

This lathe is excellent for small production work, but it can also handle large blocks up to about 88 lb. (40 kg) with ease. Bed extensions are available for long work.

If you want to turn heavy long spindles, you'll need a long-bed lathe like this Vicmarc model.

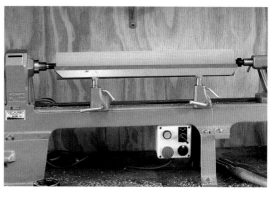

A long tool rest reduces setup time when turning long spindles.

A lathe with a 12-in. (305mm) swing—like those at the *left* and *rear*—is all most turners ever need. For small work, a mini-lathe (*right*) is perfectly adequate.

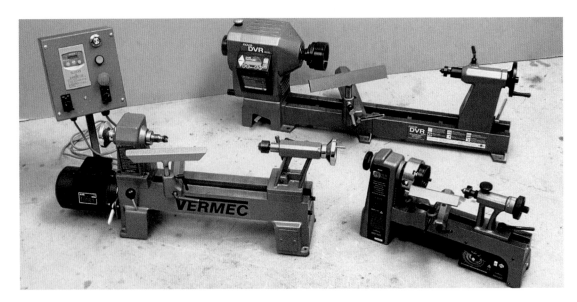

A swivel-head lathe allows easier access for hollowing enclosed forms and can hold larger diameter jobs than those that fit over the bed.

Pedestal lathes allow you to work across the lathe axis when hollowing.

My observation is that most turners work well within the capacity of a midsize lathe that swings 12 in. to 16 in. (300mm to 400mm). If you are unlikely to turn diameters greater than 6 in. (150mm), a mini-lathe is probably all you'll need.

Some midsize lathes have a swivel head-stock, which enables you to work more comfortably when hollowing enclosed forms. They also allow you to turn larger diameter work than you would be able to mount over the bed. The disadvantage of a swivel head-stock is that you can't use the tail center when the head is swiveled.

Pedestal lathes also enable you to work comfortably across the axis of the lathe when turning bowls and hollowing enclosed forms.

If your interest is in projects measured in feet rather than inches, in meters rather than centimeters, there are very substantial lathes available. However, these are too slow and cumbersome for small-scale turning and are not ideal to learn on.

Very large lathes, designed for large and heavy projects, are not well suited to turning small-scale work.

This shopmade lathe is basic, does the job superbly, and costs very little to construct.

Top-quality lathes are expensive, but they tend to retain their value. If you are on a tight budget, have specific requirements, or simply enjoy doing it, constructing your own lathe is a good option. In Wales, Mike Scott turns massive lumps of timber on a very simple but strong lathe made of steel I-beams welded together beneath a slab of 1-in. (25mm) plate. The faceplate has added ribs for strength. A more sophisticated shop-built lathe I encountered in Canberra, Australia, is modeled on a standard lathe.

If you wish to keep fit as you turn, you can build yourself the sort of foot-powered pole or treadle lathe on which wood turners used to earn a living.

Lathes used to be constructed on site. Englishman Robin Wood earns a living turning bowls on his traditional foot-powered pole lathe.

Lathe Attachments

A new lathe usually comes with a faceplate, a spur drive, and a tail center. These basic mounting devices will get you started, but there are other accessories that will make turning everything except spindles a whole lot easier and more enjoyable. I'll discuss these holding devices briefly here, but they'll be covered in more detail in Section Eight (p. 71).

To turn wood you need to fix it securely on the lathe, and you want to be able to do this quickly and easily in a way that doesn't compromise the design of your object. There are three basic strategies for fixing wood on a lathe: blanks can be pinned between centers, screwed to a faceplate, or held in a chuck.

A blank is most simply mounted between centers. Power is transmitted to the wood via prongs on the spur drive, and the blank is kept pressed against the drive by the tail center. A drive cannot be used without a tail center.

Drives and centers come in various sizes, as shown above. The type of drive center you

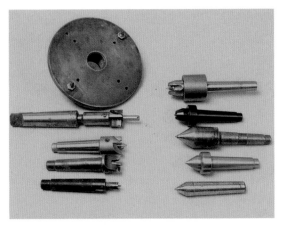

Blanks can be mounted between spur drives (*left*) and centers (*right*). The spur faceplate drive (*top*) is for large bowl blanks, and the mandrel drive immediately below it is for lamp bases.

use will depend on the scale, weight, and nature of the blank. For example, a $^3/_8$-in. (9mm) drive is ideal for small projects like lace bobbins and pens, but for a typical baluster you'll need the standard 1-in. (25mm) diameter. A large-spur faceplate is for natural-edge bowls and large face work, whereas a mandrel drive is for lamp bases.

Tail centers also come in a range of styles for different diameter workpieces and varying situations. A revolving center with a bearing is highly recommended, although you can manage with a plain (solid) conical center. Most of the time I use a conical tail center for very small jobs and a cup center for everything else. Again, purchase variations only as you need them.

Faceplates are used to hold face-work blanks. Plain faceplates are attached to blanks off the lathe with screws. However, center screw faceplates (usually called screw chucks) are much quicker and easier to use. You can make your own. First screw a disc

Most lathes come equipped with the basic means of fixing wood: a faceplate, a drive center, and a tail center.

A variety of faceplates are available for holding face-work blanks. The blanks are screwed to plain metal faceplates through holes in the plate. However, center screw faceplates (also called screw chucks) are much quicker and easier to use. You can also make your own screw chuck.

about 1 in. (25mm) thick to a standard faceplate, true it, and make the face slightly concave. Drill a small hole through the disc at the center; then, from the back, insert a screw long enough to project about ¾ in. (20mm) from the face. See *Turning Wood* (Taunton, 2001) or *Turning Bowls* (Taunton, 2002) for information about making your own screw chuck.

If you are turning more than just spindles, a self-centering four-jaw chuck is essential. A four-jaw chuck incorporates four slides to which a variety of jaws can be fitted. A chuck typically comes with one set of jaws, but you'll often be better off using a different set of jaws that is more suited for the work you are doing. As a bowl turner, I use step jaws most of the time, but for all end-grain projects, like boxes, I use the standard or longer jaws. The advantages of these chucks are that they grip both square and round blanks securely and they grip by expanding within a space or rebate or by clamping around a foot or tenon.

A cup chuck is essentially a cylindrical hole in a lump of metal into which turned blanks are driven with a mallet. Traditionally used for production of end-grain work, these days they have been superseded by mechanical chucks. I use the body of an outdated chuck, but you can make one yourself by welding a

Four-jaw chucks are available in a variety of models and can accept various jaws suited to particular types of work.

A cup chuck is an inexpensive option for holding end-grain blanks. This is an old chuck body.

A three-point "steady" keeps long center work and deep hollowed work from whipping on the lathe.

Steadies are usually shopmade for specific jobs. This one is for spindles.

short length of cylindrical steel tube over a substantial nut. Look in flea markets and clearance sales for old chucks you might be able to use, but be sure they'll fit your lathe's spindle, either directly or with an adapter.

Center steadies are designed to keep long, small-diameter spindles spinning true without any whip, but they are even better for supporting deep vases as they are hollowed. Each lathe manufacturer offers a center steady, but turners traditionally make their own for specific jobs.

Shaping Tools

Choose HSS tools rather than carbon steel, and turn varying handles to help identify tools on the bench.

A BEWILDERING NUMBER OF TURNING tools are available commercially. Most are variations on the standard gouges, scrapers, and chisels that have developed over the centuries. There are many specialist tools made by individuals, which will probably disappear when their makers retire or die, so I've decided not to deal with these specifically. A lot of this is deep-hollowing and off-center gear that works well, but it's exceedingly difficult to provide ongoing sources for it. And many people make their own version anyway.

Nearly all turning tools are now made of high-speed steel (HSS), which wears much better than the carbon steels used formerly. Each of the three major divisions of woodturning—center work, face work, and endgrain hollowing—require a slightly different set of tools, although there is some overlap.

The range of tools you possess should reflect what you turn on your lathe. If your interest is spindle turning, you will want a skew chisel and maybe five other tools, but no deep-fluted bowl gouges. If you want to turn only bowls you'll need several gouges and a few scrapers, but no skew chisel. Shallow gouges are useful for both spindle and face work. For turning the insides of hollow forms, you'll need yet another clutch of hollowing tools.

It is all too easy to collect tools you use once or never. Unless you are a tool junkie, I advise purchasing tools only as you need them. It's wise to try them out first, or at least talk to someone who has used them or who knows about them. If there is a wood-turning group in your area, it should be a good source of information.

When you begin to purchase turning tools you'll soon notice that some are much thicker and heavier than others. The strength of the thicker tools is essential when the tool overhangs the rest more than a couple of inches (50mm). Gouges and skew chisels should be at least ¼ in. (6mm) thick and long scrapers should be ⅜ in. (9mm) thick. However, tools more than ½ in. (13mm) thick can be difficult to use effectively on small projects.

Tools for Center Work

In center work, the grain of the wood is aligned parallel to the lathe axis. Typical center work includes chair parts, drawer knobs, light pulls, baluster spindles, and tool handles. The photo above right shows a set of basic center-work tools.

A roughing gouge is used to turn rough or square-section blanks to round. Roughing gouges can be shallow or deep fluted. Both work equally well.

Center-work tools commonly include (*from left*) a parting tool, a roughing gouge, a skew chisel, and various spindle gouges.

Spindle gouges always have shallow, rounded flutes and long fingernail ends. A detail gouge—designed to cut deep and narrow coves—has a very shallow, rounded flute.

A parting tool is used for establishing diameters and for *parting off*, which means cutting right down to the center of the piece to separate a section or complete a job.

The skew chisel is *the* finishing tool to use on any spindle, and it's used to turn cylinders, V-grooves, beads, and long concave curves. The skew is regarded as the most difficult turning tool to use, but you can get a superior finish straight off the tool, so it's worth mastering. The size of skew you use will depend partly on the diameter of the spindle you are turning. A ¾-in. (19mm) skew is good for general use. Wider chisels can be used on small diameters, whereas narrow chisels are more likely to catch when turning larger-diameter work.

Oval skew chisels have been widely promoted. They are excellent for planing cylinders and long curves, but you can do a lot more with a traditional rectangular section skew.

Tools for End Grain

For end-grain turnings, the grain is aligned parallel to the lathe axis, as with center work. Typical end-grain projects include boxes, pencil pots, and pepper mills. The outside profile of an end-grain project is turned using center-work tools.

How you hollow end grain depends on the diameter of the job, the diameter of the opening through which you are hollowing,

and the depth to which you are hollowing. The greater the depth, the longer and stronger the tool needs to be.

To hollow up to 4 in. (100mm) deep into end grain through a wide opening, you'll need a drill to set the depth, a spindle gouge with a fingernail edge to remove the bulk of the waste, and scrapers of varying shapes to refine the surfaces and shape.

Large-scale deep hollows of 8 in. (200mm) or more require heavier tools with long, heavy handles to control the leverage. Steel or aluminum tube is favored for long handles because they can be filled with lead shot or sand to increase the weight and dampen vibration. Also excellent are the lighter-weight Stewart system arm-brace and pistol-grip handles, shown in the photo below right. Many deep-hollowing tools have small scrapers that can be adjusted on the end of long shafts so you can undercut rims.

End-grain hollowing tools include (*from left*) a square-end scraper, round-nose scrapers, spindle gouges, and a depth drill.

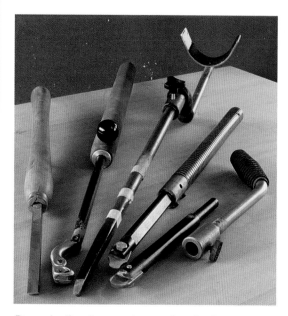

Deep-hollowing tools need to be long and strong or have a Stewart system arm-brace (*center*) or pistol-grip handle (*right*).

Bent scrapers enable you to hollow out vase forms with small openings.

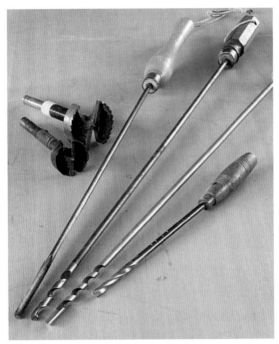

Forstner or multispur bits (*left*) will bore large-diameter holes in items such as pepper mills and hollow forms. Long drills and augers (*center*) are used for drilling out lamp bases. Many holes can be bored freehand on the lathe using a depth drill (*right*).

These are easy to make yourself. And tools based on guarded ring cutters (such as the green-handled Munro hollower in the right photo on p. 17) have been developed to shear cut without catastrophic catches.

Hollow forms are vases and vessels with very small openings of 1 in. (25mm) to 2 in. (50mm) in diameter. These enclosed forms can often be hollowed using narrow conventional scrapers. However, "squashed" forms with an undercut rim can't be reached by straight tools, so require offset cutters or bent hollowing tools. These are best mounted in heavy handles.

Deep-hollowing systems and offset scrapers are now available commercially, but until recently those interested in deep hollowing made their own tools by slot fitting HSS cutters into the ends of iron bars, which were in turn fitted into a handle.

A variety of drills can be used in or through the tailstock. Forstner or multispur bits held in a drill chuck fixed in the lathe tailstock are used for boring wide and deep cylindrical holes in things like pepper mills and kaleidoscopes. They can also be used to remove the center waste from hollow forms. Longer holes are bored using an auger inserted through a hollow tail center. Many holes can be bored freehand using a depth drill as the wood spins on the lathe.

Tools for Face Work

In face work, the grain runs at 90 degrees to the lathe axis. Typical face work includes bowls, platters, clocks, coasters, cheese boards, and trophy bases.

Face work should be turned with gouges, using scrapers to refine the surface as required. A basic face-work kit should include a ½-in. (13mm) shallow spindle gouge for roughing cuts close to the rest. A ³⁄₈-in. (9mm) spindle gouge is the best tool for cutting beads, coves, and feet. Deep-fluted bowl gouges are more heavily constructed and designed for hollowing and cutting with the tool extended well past the rest. If you intend working small scale only—say diameters less than 6 in. (150mm)—you'll need only a ³⁄₈-in. (9mm) gouge. For larger-diameter work, use a long and strong ½-in.-(13mm-) deep, fluted bowl gouge. The best scrapers for bowl work are radiused rather than round nose.

If you are turning bowls, you'll find shear scrapers handy for cleaning up end grain and getting clean cuts in corners where gouges can't always reach. Because shear scrapers are used tilted on edge, the blades have rounded sides to help them slide easily along a rest. It's simple to make your own from older scrapers that are too short for general work. Use a disc or belt sander to round over the sides of a spear-point scraper or just the lower side of a skewed scraper.

Shaped scrapers are available in different sizes to make cutting beads or loose rings easy.

> ⚠ **WARNING** Do not use old files as scrapers because they can snap if you have a heavy catch.

Basic face-work tools include (*from left*) a chuck-recess scraper, shallow gouges, bowl gouges, a square-end scraper, and bowl scrapers.

Shear scrapers are good for smoothing and refining face work and getting into corners.

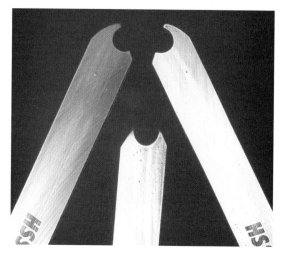

Beading scrapers make turning repetitious beads and rings easy.

"Bowl-saving" systems like the Stewart system slicer (*left*) and the McNaughton system cutters (*right*) can be used to extract the center from a bowl blank for a smaller project or projects.

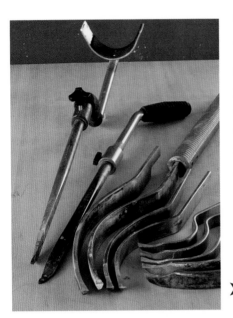

Wood-Saving Tools

Various "bowl-saving" systems can be used to extract the center of open bowls on smaller projects. The simplest systems are straight slicers like the Stewart system slicer, which enables you to extract conical lumps and rough bowls. It also allows you to turn rings for frames. More sophisticated systems, like the McNaughton system, have gates to prevent parabolic or hemispherical cutters from catching.

▶ See *"Nesting Bowls"* on p. 214.

Shaping Tools for the Lathe

Tool	Uses/Applications
Gouge, roughing: ¾"–2" (20mm–50mm)	Roughing down center work only
Gouge, shallow and detail: < 1/2" (< 13mm)	Turning detail on spindles and face work; hollowing end grain
Gouge, shallow: ½" (13mm)	Center-work coves; roughing bowl profiles; roughing small center work; hollowing end grain
Gouge, deep fluted: up to ⅝" (16mm)	Bowls; particularly hollowing
Skew chisel	Center work only
Scraper, square-end	Hollowing end grain; face-work recesses; scraping convex curves; hollowing end grain and face work
Scraper, straight-edge skew	Finishing bowl profiles
Scraper, radiused skew	Finishing inside bowls; concave face work
Scraper, round-nose	End-grain hollowing; shear scraping face-work coves
Scraper, spear point	Shear scraping face-work corners; cutting grooves
Scraper, bent	Hollowing forms with small openings
Scraper, side and formed	Undercutting rims; end-grain hollowing
Scraper, dovetailed	Dovetailing recesses for expanding chucks
Parting tool, < ⅛" (3mm)	Parting off small-diameter center work
Parting tool, other	Sizing center work; parting off center work
Boring bar, with high-speed steel cutters	Hollowing hollow forms
Hollowing system	Hollowing deep vessels and forms

Ancillary Tools

YOU NEED MORE THAN A LATHE and a couple of gouges to turn wood. This section deals with items that make turning safer, easier, and more enjoyable—saving you time, money, and material.

For instance, you can purchase prepared blanks, but you have more control over grain alignment and more fun when cutting your own, so you need at least one saw. You also need measuring tools to lay out your blanks and to measure your work at it progresses. Sharp tools are essential, so you must have a grinder, a wheel dresser to go with it, and possibly a grinding jig to get you started.

This section considers other tools like cordless drills, which are not essential but can make life a lot easier, and chainsaws, which enable you to cast a predatory eye well beyond your local timber dealer.

You also need safety equipment. Wood spinning on the lathe does explode from time to time, so you need to guard against this inevitability and against the fine dust that is part of woodturning.

Safety and Dust Extraction

There are two major safety concerns for a woodturner: dust and flying debris. Fortunately there is equipment available to protect you from both.

Dust is a major fire and health hazard in any woodshop. For woodturners, some sort of dust extraction at the lathe is essential; you need a dust collector. When buying a dust collector, bigger is generally better. However, I recommend, as a minimum, a system that is capable of moving about 650 cu. ft. of air per minute (cfm). Many single-stage dust collectors are capable of this and are quite affordable. To maximize dust collection at its source, connect the dust collector to a collection hood at the lathe (see photos on p. 45).

Very fine, suspended dust particles can be collected using a ceiling-hung ambient-air cleaner with microfilters. However, where the climate allows, a breeze through open doors probably does an even better job.

Aside from dust and chips, blanks will occasionally fly off the lathe or explode

The pleated filters within the cylindrical mesh top of this dust collector filter out dust down to 5 microns before recycling the air back into the workspace.

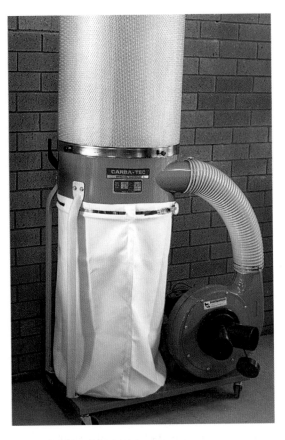

during turning. You always need to be prepared for an event like this because it's not a question of if it will happen, but when. Sometimes woodturners don't wear protection because a particular procedure "will only take a second." Unfortunately, this is often when accidents happen. Such carelessness is regularly noted in woodturning magazines, so take care. Nearly every turner I know is a scar-bearing statistic.

Most professional studio turners spend their time at the lathe wearing an impact-resistant respirator helmet that filters the air they breath. Such a helmet provides a positive airflow across your face, preventing misting of the shield or eyeglasses. Before buying this sort of face protection, ensure that the visor can be easily tipped up for conversations and job inspections. Otherwise, removing the whole helmet soon becomes tedious.

A face shield or a pair of safety glasses (*left*) offer basic eye protection, and filter masks (*center*) protect your lungs. However, a respirator helmet (*right*) is best because it provides face protection as well as filtered air.

If you opt not to use a face shield when turning small items, at least wear safety glasses. Replacement eye technology is not yet up and running.

Tools for Sharpening

Woodturning, like any woodworking, is much easier with sharp tools. And blunt tools are hazardous in that they encourage dangerous tool handling. Tool edges are shaped and sharpened using a grinder. You can grind at higher speeds using a dry wheel or more slowly and safely using a water-cooled system.

Typical high-speed dry grinders run at about 3600 rpm, are universally available, and are inexpensive. However a better, although more expensive, option is a grinder that runs at around 1725 rpm, a speed at which you are less likely to burn your tool edges. There are some wonderful industrial grinders with wheels in excess of 10 in. (255mm) in diameter, which give you a shallower concave bevel, but these cost a lot more. Most turners now grind on an 8-in. (200mm) grinder. You'll need adjustable rests that can be readily set to the angle required for the tool being ground. If these don't come fitted with your grinder, you can buy them as aftermarket accessories like the O'Donnell and Heligrind rests shown in the photo above.

If you are a novice turner, you might want to consider one of the numerous

Dry-wheel grinders are commonly available and relatively inexpensive. A good wheel dresser (*front left*) is essential, and diamond honing sticks and an oilstone (*front right*) are also useful in the sharpening process.

> **⚠ WARNING** Grinding can be a dangerous process, so wear eye protection at all times.

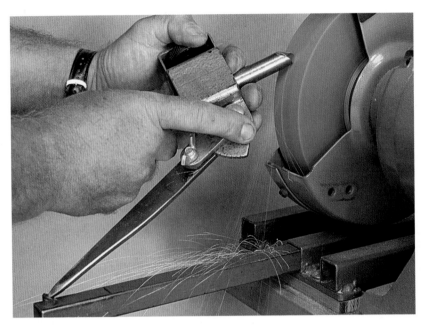

A grinding jig can help you learn how to sharpen gouges properly.

Though slower cutting than a dry wheel, a water-cooled grinder such as this Tormek™ will prevent burning a tool edge when sharpening.

commercially available grinding jigs. Such a jig is a great aid when learning how to grind. However, in the long run, I suggest learning how to grind gouges freehand because it's faster and more satisfying. Also, jigs impose an edge/bevel combination on the tool that is rarely ideal.

Set up your grinder with a 36-grit wheel for coarse grinding and shaping and a 60-grit wheel from which you can take the edge straight to work on the lathe. Most turning tools are now made of high-speed steel (HSS), which is best ground using a white, friable aluminum oxide wheel or ceramic wheel (available from specialist woodturning stores). The standard gray wheels supplied with most grinders will do the job, but not as efficiently. You'll need a wheel dresser to keep the wheels in shape and free of the metal particles that accumulate during grinding. Wide diamond wheel dressers are far superior to all others.

You can obtain a superior edge using a water-cooled wheel. Although grinding is slower, you'll never burn the edge. It's best to have both types of grinders. That way you can quickly rough grind on a high-speed dry wheel before moving to the water-cooled wheel to complete the job. A water wheel is incredibly useful for flattening the tops of scrapers and thread chasers, as well as sharpening kitchen knives.

Although turning tools are generally used straight off the grinder, diamond honing sticks and oilstones can be used to hone an edge to ultimate sharpness, to remove burrs, and to polish tool flutes and tops before grinding.

▶ See *"Preparing Tools for Grinding"* on p. 84.
See *"Honing"* on p. 92.

Wood Preparation Tools

There are companies that sell turning blanks for bowls, chess sets, pens, boxes, and other projects, but buying from them is an expensive way to purchase wood. Worse yet, you have no say in precisely how the wood is cut. It's better to buy logs or boards from which to cut your own blanks.

Of course you'll need a saw to cut your own blanks. Most woodturners use a bandsaw and/or a table saw for this purpose. A bandsaw is by far the most useful saw for most woodturners. It will allow you to cut cylindrical bowl blanks from sawn boards and to prepare little chunks for small projects. Even a good-quality hobby bandsaw can be used to break down small logs.

For spindle blanks, which need to be square in cross section, you'll need a table

Various portable saws enable you to break down timber into manageable sizes.

A bandsaw (*rear*) is essential for cutting face-work blanks. A table saw (*front*) does a quicker, more accurate job of preparing center-work squares.

saw, which cuts more accurately and with greater speed than a bandsaw.

For larger logs, you'll need a chainsaw. For indoor use, an electric saw is preferable because it produces no fumes and is relatively quiet. In the great outdoors, away from electricity, you'll need a gas-powered saw. I have also found a portable circular saw to be useful for crosscutting boards when preparing platter blanks from boards that are too wide to crosscut on my bandsaw. These days, though, I use my electric chainsaw for that. I also keep a bowsaw in the car for crosscutting small branches.

Tools for Measuring

In addition to tools used for marking out blanks, you'll often need others for measuring job diameters, wall thickness, or depth as work proceeds.

For turning spindles, you can survive with a ruler, pencil, and standard spring calipers. However, I also find Vernier calipers and

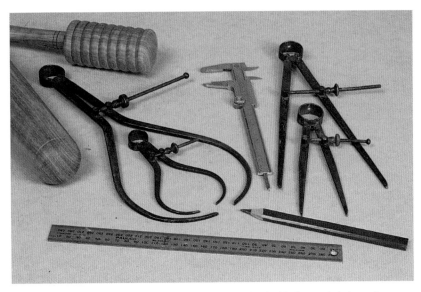

Center-work measuring tools should include (*left to right*) spring calipers, ruler, vernier calipers, and dividers.

For end-grain hollowing, add to your center-work measuring tools a depth drill and set of internal spring calipers (*far right*) for measuring enclosed diameters.

For face-work, your collection of measuring tools should include (*clockwise from top left*) double-ended calipers, straight-arm calipers, dividers, depth drill, ruler, and square.

dividers very useful for laying out details. I round over the nose of the jaws of Vernier calipers so they don't catch when sizing a rotating spindle.

For small end-grain projects like boxes, the same kit will work, but with the addition of internal spring calipers and a depth drill.

A face-work measuring kit should include dividers for marking out blanks and for measuring diameters as work proceeds. Double-ended calipers enable you to measure wall thickness on bowls. Straight-arm calipers let you measure the base on wide shallow jobs as well as the wall on a deep narrow form. A depth drill sets the depth to which you will hollow. Depth can be further checked using a rule and square.

Drills

You will find both conventional and angle drills useful in woodturning, especially for bowl work and large face work. A drill press works well for drilling holes in blanks in preparation for mounting, although a cordless drill is handier. Conventional handheld drills are also used for power sanding, but an angle drill is easier to handle and far superior for this purpose. Cordless drills lack the power required for power sanding.

You can use a drill press to drill holes for attaching face-work blanks to a screw faceplate. A cordless drill is more convenient but less accurate.

Sanding and Finishing

Abrasives for finishing are available in sheets and rolls. The best are backed with lightweight cloth that is flexible and easy to tear into usable portions.

Most face work is now power sanded using drills outfitted with foam pads on which are mounted abrasive discs. The discs can be purchased, but they are easy to punch out using a wad punch—an ideal activity for those days when you need to relieve your stress level.

Nonelectric rotary sanders are also excellent finishing tools and virtually eliminate sanding marks. These ingenious little devices simply consist of a freewheeling disc attached to a handle. Pressing the abrasive-faced disk to a spinning job causes the disk to spin, sanding the piece.

Most face work is power sanded using drills outfitted with foam-backed abrasive discs. The discs are available commercially but can also be created using a wad punch (*far left*). Nonelectric rotary sanders (*right front*) can produce scratch-free surfaces.

Wood

WOOD IS EXTRACTED FROM living organisms—trees. The very best wood comes from the heartwood of living trees chopped down in their prime. Trees that die slowly through disease or the rot of old age never yield timber of equal quality or workability. Sapwood, which is usually paler than the heartwood and more subject to insect attack, was traditionally discarded. However, because quality timber is becoming an increasingly scarce resource, all parts of a tree are often used these days, especially by studio woodturners.

Wood is rarely a stable material, so when you start using it or stashing it away for future use, you need to be aware of what it's likely to do as it gets older. A growing tree contains lots of water; in fact, you'll get very wet turning freshly felled wood. But the moment a tree has been felled, it begins to dry out. As the water leaves the cells, the wood shrivels and shrinks until it reaches equilibrium with its environment, at which point it is considered *seasoned*. If seasoned wood is then moved to a dryer environment

it will shrink further. Or if it's moved to damper conditions, it will expand. Most people are familiar with doors or drawers that tighten in humid months, then become loose in the dry months.

The seasoning of timber can happen naturally over time (called *air drying*) or it can be hastened by using a kiln (called *kiln drying*.) The traditional rule of thumb for air drying is 1 year per inch (25mm) plus 1 year. So, theoretically, the stack of 2½-in.- (65mm-) thick elm boards shown in the photo opposite top left will take about 3½ years to air dry. However, some timbers dry much more quickly, while others take considerably longer.

The longer you air dry wood, the better it is to work: 30-year-old wood is better than wood just 3 years sawn, while I've found that 300-year-old wood is better still. (You might find some.) For jobs like boxes, bowls, and vases that will be hollowed, you can speed the air drying process by rough turning—a process whereby you roughly shape your bowl, box, or vase oversize to

This slabbed elm log is being naturally air dried. The wooden stickers separating the slabs allow air circulation.

reduce the drying time. The rule of thumb is to turn the job to about 15 percent of the size of the finished project. For example, the walls on a 10-in.- (250mm-) diameter bowl should be rough turned to about 1½ in. (40mm) thick.

Kilns will dry wood in a few weeks, but the wood is more expensive than air-dried wood and not as nice to work. Despite this, kiln-dried wood will mostly be used for jobs where there is no hollowing, like baluster spindles or knobs.

Where to Find Wood

Wood is commercially available from sawmills, timber dealers, do-it-yourself stores, and woodturning supply companies. If you're a novice turner, you'll find stores and mail-order catalogs that cater to woodturners useful in getting you started. Along with tools, these companies often stock a range of blanks and timber, often including exotic woods not found in hardware stores.

To speed the seasoning of wood, jobs can be rough turned oversize, then left to dry before the final turning.

Specialist woodturning stores, like this one in Calgary, offer a range of blanks cut especially for woodturners.

These are mostly small businesses run by ex-woodworkers and turners who can offer excellent advice based on their own experience. Many offer courses to help get you started.

Sawmills and large lumber dealers are typically not very interested in small orders. However, some mills have offcut bins from which they sell lumps and boards that are useless for joinery but excellent for turnery.

Wood can be purchased freshly felled, kiln dried, air dried, or partly seasoned. Although you can buy wood presawn into blanks, bowl and vase turners tend to favor logs, billets, and lumps. Most expensive are

This timber in a sawmill's scrap shed is useless for cabinetmaking but will yield many excellent turning blanks.

Bowl material like small burls (*left*) go straight on the lathe, whereas larger pieces are slabbed first (*right*).

This wood was commercially prepared to be sold as blanks for boxes, end-grain jobs, and bowls. The highly figured blanks (*top center*) were waxed to prevent splitting.

turning blanks, which should be free of defects but often are not. The drier the wood is and the farther it is, both geographically and metaphorically, from the original tree, the more expensive it will be. Bowl blanks sawn from green (freshly felled) timber are usually sealed with wax to limit splitting.

Most boards sold are less than 3 in. (75mm) thick. Those thicker are rarely wider than 8 in. (200mm). Timber is cut primarily for building and furniture, so a spindle turner will have no problem finding suitable material, but wood for larger face work, like bowls and platters, is not so readily available.

There is a great deal of timber lying around that provides wonderful practice material. Demolition and building sites can yield enormous quantities, particularly for spindles, but make sure to check it for nails, screws, and other hardware.

In urban areas, trees are constantly being pruned and felled, so it pays to keep an eye on your local parks and gardens, as well as neighbors' backyards. Arborists often maintain a yard full of logs for recycling. I've found that many slow-growing small trees and ornamental shrubs provide excellent box material that never splits.

If you are lucky enough to live near forest or woodlands, you might get permission to scavenge among the debris left by commercial loggers. Because they prefer to cut cylindrical logs that yield clean defect-free boards, loggers tend to leave crotches and smaller limbs in the forest floor. And these are the portions of a tree that non-spindle turners find most interesting.

For face-work projects, you can make good use of material that most other woodworkers regard as waste. I know of one pool table manufacturer who delivers several pallets of large maple offcuts to a woodturning school every week because it's more efficient than taking it to the dump. Small joinery shops always have quantities of fully seasoned offcuts that can be glued up to form larger blanks.

Before you grab any log that's offered to you, know what you want to do with it and where you are going to put it. Over the years, I have seen hundreds of tons of formerly good timber rendered useless—sometimes in days—from being left in the sun. When you get hold of logs, cut them into boards or blanks as soon as possible. Make sure to coat the end grain with wax to limit splitting. Bowl turners should rough turn logs as soon as possible to get the maximum from a tree.

Selecting Wood

When it comes to selecting wood, there is no substitute for experience. Buying wood is often something of a lottery, especially if it has been bleached silvery gray from lying around for years exposed to daylight. You might get a hint of the heartwood color on the end grain of freshly cut timber, but after only a few weeks this becomes obscure. As you get excited about bright and flashy grain, it's well to remember that, in the long run, most woods fade to gold and dark brown in ambient light. Any wood exposed to direct sun and the elements will go silver.

When the end of a log shows splits, reckon on losing at least 6 in. to 8 in. (150mm to 200mm) before you are free of end-grain defects and into mostly solid wood. Major splits can run the entire length of a log.

Wood darkens quickly. In only a couple of weeks, the lighter, fresh-cut surfaces will match the dark triangle at bottom right, which was cut 2 weeks earlier.

A prime advantage of purchasing sawn timber is that you can see the grain patterns on each face. However, on a weathered or aged board you'll need to scrape or plane a small section to reveal the grain, then wet the surface to bring out the color. Although wetting the surface with oil is preferable, it's usually not available when you're on the move. Instead, the usual practice is to spit on the board and rub that in. Some fiddleback and quilting figure in wood can be confused with saw marks or can be difficult to spot beneath the waxed surface.

Any tree with a fluted, knobby, or lumpy trunk is likely to yield interesting wavy or bird's-eye grain patterns. A crotch will have a feathery figure and can often be slabbed thin enough to make several dishes or small

Reckon to lose at least 6 in. to 8 in. (150mm to 200mm) from the end of a log before you reach wood that is free of all but the largest splits.

The surface of this blackened New Guinea rosewood board was sanded to reveal the grain and color of the board.

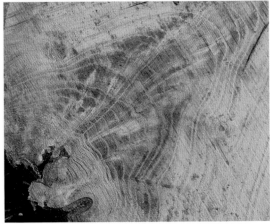

When sawn, the gnarled mulberry log (*top*) revealed interesting grain with feathery crotch patterns (*bottom*).

A dramatic, open-grained eucalyptus burl like this is, for safety, better worked thick than thin.

Rays parallel to the cut face yield a ribbon figure.

Corrugations on a tree (left) indicate highly figured wood within (right).

trays. Rough burls can be slabbed to make wonderful platter blanks, although the structure of some burl is more suitable for chunky forms than for thin-walled vessels.

Some timbers have strong rays visible on the end grain, radiating from the pith. If boards are quartersawn with the broad faces parallel to the radial rays, you get a ribbon pattern that is spectacular on flat objects like

trays. You need very large trees to obtain wide, flawless boards, as the pith is usually split.

Corrugations on a tree, often on the underside of branches, are an indication of fiddleback patterns. In species like ash and maple you occasionally find logs with one full side exhibiting solid figure.

Holes in the sap-wood of this walnut log indicate wood-worm activity.

Recognizing Defects and Problems

As with many things in life, the best is often found on the fringe of disaster or catastrophe. For example, some of the most colorful wood occurs because of incipient rot or beetle attack. Also, most twisted, swirling grain is highly stressed and likely to split.

If you notice dust as you sift through a stack of boards, you've found indication of active borers—either woodworm or termites. Woodworm is usually found in sapwood, although the occasional adventurous bug does wander off into the hardwood to ruin an otherwise excellent log or board. Rather than leaving holes, termites tend to chew away whole areas of wood. If there are holes but no dust, chances are the bugs are gone, so you can consider filling odd holes rather than discarding a whole board.

Areas of rot are soft and often pale. Look for discolored sections in otherwise sound timber to ascertain its extent.

It's important to check the end of a log for splits. Splits along growth rings, called

Dust on a board indicates wood-worm or termite activity. The large chewed areas seen here are signs of termites.

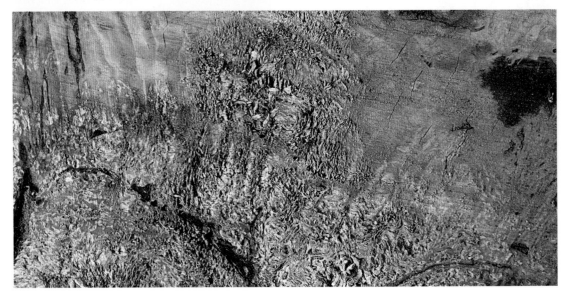

Rot is often whitish and pulpy.

cup shakes, severely limit the size of clean blanks you can cut.

Areas of wood that are likely to be particularly difficult to cut cleanly will be hairy, almost like a coconut husk or coir mat. However, this sort of grain can be a sign of spectacular highlights, so the difficulties of obtaining a cleanly cut surface may be rewarded. Fissures are worth avoiding, as they can indicate cavelike systems in the wood. That said, a lot of fissures can lead to a decorative turning. If the adjacent figure is very nice, you can make the holes look like black knots, filling them with black dust set in a cyanoacrylate adhesive.

► See *"Repairing Knots and Splits"* on p. 233.

Many of the more interesting and heavy woods are currently sold by weight. A blank is priced based on its unseasoned weight, which is often written on the surface. The actual weight might be half, indicating that the wood has dried, or nearly so.

The big split to the right of the white sap is a cup shake on a growth ring, the sort of defect that severely limits the size of clean blanks you can cut.

Furry tufts and hairy grain (*left*) indicate wood that can be difficult to work. Avoid fissured timber (*right*) unless it's bad enough to be decorative.

Setting Up the Lathe, page 38

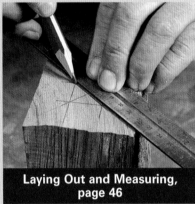
Laying Out and Measuring, page 46

Preparing Blanks, page 58

Fixing Wood on the Lathe, page 71

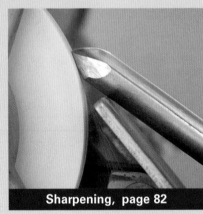
Sharpening, page 82

PART TWO

Preparation

MANY PEOPLE GIVE UP WOODTURNING almost before they've started, never realizing that their badly set up lathe and poorly sharpened tools never gave them a chance. With tenacity, you can turn tough lumps of wood on a rattling second-rate lathe using blunt tools in a mess of a workshop, but it's not much fun. And you increase the risk of serious injury.

With a bit of effort, you can get your lathe properly set up and your workspace well ordered. Although wonderful work can be created with next to no ancillary equipment, turning is much easier with modern chucks, tools, and grinding jigs that introduce you to a sharp edge.

A good working environment makes life easier and more enjoyable. Investing in good chucks and other ancillary equipment and learning how to best use them pays endless dividends. So does learning about your raw material and how to select the blanks best suited to your projects.

Setting Up the Lathe

WHEN YOU SPIN A ROUGH BLANK on a lathe, most lathes will vibrate somewhat, and light-weight models will shimmy across the floor or bench if not anchored down. I bolted my first lathe to a thick board which was clamped to a metal table. This lathe had too high a low speed (about 900 rpm), so I learned to lean against the machine and to keep the tools pressed against my side as I combated the vibration. Fortunately, the cobbled floor prevented my having to follow the lathe across the room as I turned blanks to round. Ever since, my lathes have been on very substantial stands anchored to a thick concrete floor and are capable of much lower speeds.

Time spent setting up and tuning your lathe is time well spent. Once you've experienced vibration-free turning or used a tool rest that seems to float along the bed as you reposition it, you'll be glad you made the effort.

The Workspace

It's important to set up your lathe so that your tools and abrasives are within easy reach and your grinder for sharpening is no more than a few steps away. I like a view when I look up, so I locate my lathe so I'm not facing a wall. Standing for hours on a concrete floor is tiring, so I have a large rubber mat in front of the lathe. A sheet of plywood or thin boards work as well. Dust collection hoods surround the headstock. I store my chucks in bench drawers facing the lathe and in a mobile cabinet that also holds abrasives. Measuring tools hang on the wall over the bench. A mobile tool trolley to the right of the lathe can be rolled clear to make cleaning up easier. When not in use on the lathe, the tailstock is kept on its own stand near the lathe.

[TIP] When the tailstock is not in use on the lathe, store it on its own stand at lathe-bed height to avoid back strain from lifting.

A trolley for tools and a mobile accessory cabinet are easy to roll clear for cleanup or making space for specific tasks.

When a heavy tail-stock is not in use on the lathe, keep it on its own stand, set at lathe height to prevent back strain from lifting.

The workshop itself needs good ambient lighting, but also useful is a strong adjustable lamp that can throw light from any angle around the job.

Keep your floor free of cables, blanks, and other objects that you might trip over. A nonskid surface is essential for safe working. When turning waxed blanks, the floor can become very slippery from the shavings. If you find your floor becoming slick from the wax, a short-term solution is to splash around some water or scatter sand. However, it's better to use a textured mat or board painted with deck paint. Alternatively, you could paint your floor, sprinkling sand on the wet paint as you go.

Needless to say, the lathe throws off a lot of shavings, as shown in the drawing at right. Those areas where shavings generally land should be kept clear of small tools so you don't lose them when cleaning up. I keep all my tommy bars and steel bits on magnetic bars and trays mounted on a nearby

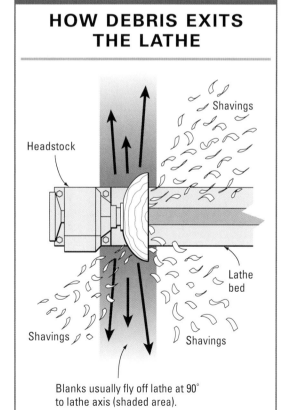

HOW DEBRIS EXITS THE LATHE

Headstock

Shavings

Shavings

Lathe bed

Shavings

Blanks usually fly off lathe at 90° to lathe axis (shaded area).

cabinet. This makes vacuuming shavings easy, as everything stays put. Nonmagnetic tools, pencils, dental picks, and such live in a pencil pot easily lifted clear for cleanup. Because shavings are a fire hazard, they should be cleaned up daily. Whenever possible, vacuum them up so as not to raise dust by sweeping.

Tuning Your Lathe

The lathe is the heart of your turning activity. The better it is set up, the more you'll be able to do on it and the more enjoyable it will be to use. Setting up a lathe properly involves aligning the centers, stabilizing the lathe, locating the belts and switches for easy access, and tuning the tool rest.

Aligning the Centers

Wood-lathe centers are notoriously inaccurate, so check the alignment of the centers before fixing any lathe to a floor or bench. If your work involves turning only between centers, having the tail center slightly out of true is no big deal. However, if you intend to

use the tail center to support work held in a chuck, the tail center must be accurately aligned.

Check the centers in two stages. First, lock the tailstock on the bed, positioning the tail center nose to nose with a spur drive. If the centers don't meet, you'll need to adjust the headstock or tailstock until they do. Some lathes include an adjustment screw on the tailstock for this purpose, but on other machines you'll have to use shims. If the tail center is low, raise it by shimming between the tailstock and the lathe bed. If the drive center is low, shim underneath the headstock. Shims can be made from pieces of aluminum cans, or you can build up layers of metal kitchen foil to make very small adjustments. If the centers are out of adjustment side to side, try adjusting the headstock alignment on the lathe bed.

Next, check the alignment halfway down the bed using a blank with smooth end grain mounted on a faceplate or in a chuck. Position the tail center lightly against the end grain and rotate the chuck by hand. If

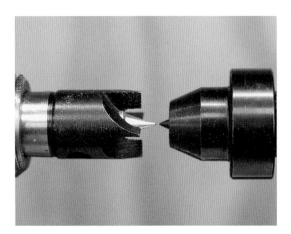

To check the alignment of the centers, begin by locating them nose to nose, with the tailstock locked to the lathe bed.

To check the alignment halfway down the bed, inspect the rotation of a chuck-mounted cylinder in relation to the tail-center point.

Use blocks or wedges to level and support the lathe before bolting it to the floor.

An ancient lathe bolted to a ton of concrete runs vibration free. The motor for this lathe is set to the rear of the headstock.

the tail center is out of true, it will leave a circle on the cylinder face. If the tail center needs a shim in one position, it will need more or less shimming elsewhere on the bed. Having centers slightly out of whack is a problem only when a job is fixed in a chuck. In many situations, you can get by using a small block of medium-density fiberboard (MDF) or plywood between the tail center and the job (see photo H on p. 80). There'll be a bit of a squeal as the flat surfaces rub, but there'll be enough support for short turning sessions.

Stabilizing the Lathe

Having checked the tailstock alignment, it's time to bolt the lathe to something solid. The more stable and rigid the lathe is, the more you'll reduce turning problems associated with vibration. However, be aware that even very substantial lathes mounted on heavy bases can be twisted out of shape when bolted to an uneven surface. Consequently, it's important to "block" the lathe

by solidly leveling it before bolting it down.

Some models have adjustable screws or pads that enable you to level and steady the lathe on an uneven floor. To block up a lathe without leveling screws, use wedges to support the machine, then bolt it into place. Wedges or blocks should fill a gap without being forced in.

For comfortable working, the centers should be at your elbow height. At just under 6 ft. (182cm) tall, I'm fortunate that my VL300 lathe is just the right height for center work. However, I prefer to turn bowls on a lower center, so then I stand on a sheet of 3/4-in.- (20mm-) thick MDF to effectively reduce the lathe height.

If a lathe is not at a comfortable height, build up as solid a platform as possible, like the Graduate lathe set on its own base of concrete in the photo at bottom on p. 100. Make sure that your floor can take the weight. Raise the lathe slightly higher than you might need, especially if more than one person will be using the lathe. You can always adjust your working height by standing on a wooden platform when necessary.

Benchtop lathes need to sit on a substantial base. A stand can easily be constructed of heavy timbers. Alternatively, you could use a heavy 3-in. (75mm) steel angle or $^3/_{16}$-in.- (5mm-) thick steel plate. If your floor can take the weight, a big block of concrete is about the steadiest base you can find. If you opt for concrete, remember to leave a couple of spaces beneath for a forklift or slings, so it can be moved when necessary.

The portable mini-lathe shown in the photo below left weighs about 57 lb. (26 kg) bare. However, the motor and a $1^1/_2$-in.- (40mm-) thick MDF panel attached to the sheet-steel base brings the weight up to 100 lb. (45 kg). It doesn't need bolting down because it's heavy enough to prevent vibration on a bench, unless the blank is very unbalanced. A similarly sized lathe can also be mounted on a stand constructed of heavy steel.

With its motor and an attached base panel, this portable mini-lathe weighs 100 lb. (45 kg), ensuring vibration-free turning for any small project.

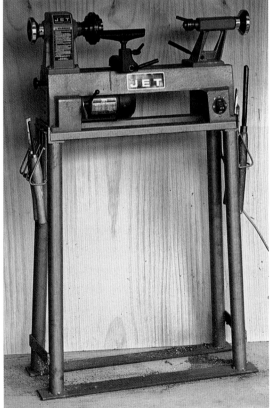

A tailor-made stand can raise a lathe to any appropriate height—like this one made by its tall owner.

LATHE STAND

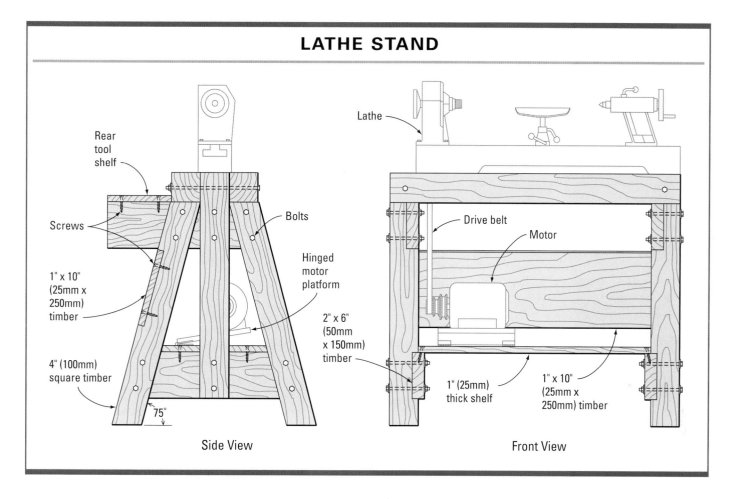

Rear tool shelf

Screws

Bolts

Hinged motor platform

1" x 10" (25mm x 250mm) timber

4" (100mm) square timber

2" x 6" (50mm x 150mm) timber

75°

Side View

Lathe

Drive belt

Motor

1" (25mm) thick shelf

1" x 10" (25mm x 250mm) timber

Front View

Locating Belts and Switches

If the headstock allows you to set the motor to the rear, adjusting the belt on step pulleys to change the lathe speed is much easier than on motors mounted below the headstock.

Ideally, your lathe should be equipped with a magnetic switch. That way, if the shop power fails and you forget to turn off the lathe, it won't automatically restart when the shop power returns. Switches should be easy to reach in case something goes wrong. A large red stop button is essential for safety. If at all possible, avoid recessed stop switches that can be operated only by hand and switches located to the rear of the headstock or lathe bed.

For maximum safety, use magnetic switches set on the front of the lathe and within easy reach as you turn.

Extended tool rests should be supported from the ground to eliminate vibration. Note also the foot-operated stop switch.

A red off bar, like those on the Vicmarc lathes shown in the photos on p. 9, is best because you don't need to use your hands at all. And there are many times when you have both hands occupied but want to cut the power. An off bar across the front of a lathe takes a few minutes to get used to, but after that you'll wonder how you ever managed without one.

When turning very large projects, a floor switch is useful because it allows you to stay as far as possible from the spinning wood.

Tuning the Tool Rest

Tool rests need to be solid. Any vibration in the rest is magnified at the cutting edge of the tool and can lead to catches. When turning large-diameter work and when using a swiveled headstock, the tool rest is often extended and poorly supported. In those cases, support it from the floor with a timber or metal post. Mike Scott's elegant solution has a threaded rod fixed to the underside of the T-rest and a matching nut welded to the end of a length of pipe, which can be screwed up and down the thread. The support is quickly adjusted by twisting the pipe.

There are few things more irritating for a turner than a sticky rest or tailstock assembly. Keep the rest in peak operational condition by daily spraying WD-40® on the bed and also under the rest assembly, then slide both the rest and tailstock along the bed to ensure they move freely. Keep the tool rest flat and smooth by regularly filing away any nicks. Many turners also wax the rest with paraffin or beeswax so the tools slide even more smoothly.

File the tool rest regularly to keep it smooth and flat.

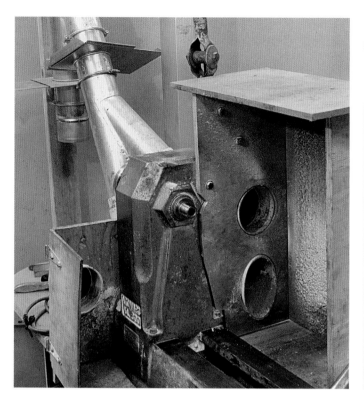
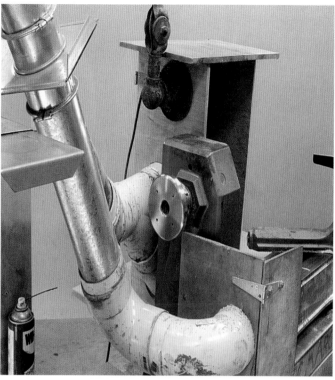

Dust Collection

In an enclosed woodworking environment, it's essential that you have efficient dust collection. Dust is a proven source of all manner of lung disease, breathing difficulties, allergies, and eczema. For years, I have spent my turning days wearing an air helmet that filters dust while providing excellent protection against the occasional exploding bowl. In addition, I avoid timbers that give me a rash or breathing difficulties. Different woods affect people differently. For example, I have no problem with the well-known irritant cocobolo, but I can't work with ebonies or with members of the *Grevillea* or *Acer* genera.

Fine airborne dust is the most dangerous for your lungs, so you should aim to collect as much of it as possible at its source. Most of this comes from sanding with abrasives, so build collection hoods around the headstock to collect the fine dust as it leaves the job. Most of my ducting is steel, with some connections made using PVC plumbing pipe. All ducting should be electrically grounded to prevent a dust explosion sparked by static electricity. If you have only a small collector, set it up for easy attachment to other machines and for daily clean up.

Dust control is a broad subject. To get your workshop properly extracted, consult a specialist publication like Sandor Nagyszalanczy's *Woodshop Dust Control* (Taunton Press, 1996).

These dust hoods are hinged to swing out of the way for specific jobs. And if a blank explodes, the rear hood is knocked clear rather than being demolished.

Laying Out
and Measuring

Laying Out

➤ Locating Center
(p. 49)

➤ Laying Out Spindles
(p. 51)

➤ Laying Out Face
Work (p. 52)

➤ Laying Out Depth
(p. 53)

Measuring

➤ Turning Specific
Diameters (p. 54)

➤ Measuring Depth
(p. 56)

➤ Measuring Thickness
(p. 57)

WOODTURNERS ARE FOREVER measuring something. We need tenons to fit holes and rebates to fit chucks. We make story battens for sets of spindles with matching diameters and details, and we constantly check wall thickness and depth when hollowing. Whenever we put a blank on the lathe, we need to know where its center is. Even when deliberately turning off center, we do so in relation to the lathe axis. And we need blanks centered to minimize waste and vibration.

Whenever possible, I prefer to rely on my eye and sense of touch in order to maintain the flow of work. The more you can do

things by eye, the better you become at it. Pinpointing the center of a disc or gauging a diameter without tools is very satisfying and it's a skill well worth developing. But it's good to double-check yourself occasionally with measuring tools, and there are times when they are simply essential.

At the very least, you'll need a pencil and a good straight-edged ruler against which to test flat and slightly dished surfaces. If you turn any form of thin-walled bowl or vessel, calipers are essential, as is a compass for accurately marking out face-work blanks. As with other tools, purchase measuring tools as you need them. I only ever used three of

A ruler is in constant use for checking flat and concave surfaces as well as for measuring.

Some of these dividers are used for laying out bowl blanks and casual measuring, but most are permanently set to specific chuck diameters.

the eight calipers I bought when I started turning. However, I've added to my collection of dividers and now have at least 20—ranging from tiny to massive—that are in constant use. Every time I go near the lathe or bandsaw, I use dividers to measure diameters and draw circles as I lay out blanks. To avoid endlessly resetting them, I keep many dividers fixed to the diameters required by my chucks.

Some measuring tools need a bit of regular attention. Divider points should be kept sharp for accurate setting out of diameters and for scratching an easily seen line when used as a compass. Caliper jaws, particularly on Vernier calipers, are best rounded so they don't catch as you gauge diameters

Keep divider points sharp by occasionally touching them up on a grinder.

Rounding over the tips of the jaws on vernier calipers prevents them catching on a spinning workpiece.

on spinning wood. Double-ended calipers seem to twist out of shape, thus requiring constant checking to ensure that both jaws meet simultaneously.

Many turners on a tight budget make their own calipers from wood or plywood, especially for unusual measuring situations when working on very deep vessels. These may work well, but they soon deteriorate with use. It's better to purchase metal rulers, calipers, and dividers. Plastic held against spinning wood wears quickly and may even melt—along with the joy of its bargain price.

▶ MEASURING INTERNAL DIAMETER

On small jobs for which the inside is wider than the opening, use internal spring calipers with outfacing points. Spin the adjustment wheel free, then wind it in until you discern pressure. Squeeze the prongs together to remove the calipers, then release the prongs to see the internal diameter. Remember: Never measure internal diameters with the lathe running.

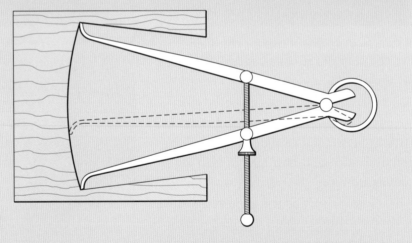

Spring-adjusted calipers retain internal measurement when withdrawn.

Locating Center

To find center on a square—typically a spindle blank—draw lines from corner to corner **(A)**. Where a corner is missing, draw lines parallel to the sides using a narrow ruler **(B)**, then draw diagonals within the resulting square or rectangle **(C)**. Faster is a center finder, which enables you to locate center on spindle blanks and cylinders by drawing a couple of intersecting lines **(D)**.

For larger diameter face-work blanks that were laid out using templates (common with commercially available discs), you might need to make your own center finder **(E)**. Use the center finder to draw three or four lines. If the lines don't intersect at the same spot, eyeball the center of the triangle or square created by the lines you drew.

You can also locate center on a disc using dividers. Set the dividers to a distance greater than the radius of the disc, then scribe intersecting arcs across the center from four points around the edge (**F**). Join the diagonal corners of the rectangle to find center (**G**). To confirm accuracy, draw as large a circle as possible centered within the arcs (**H**).

Locating center on a face-work disc is easy when laid out with a compass or dividers, both of which leave a mark at center.

To find center when the wood is spinning on the lathe, just touch a pencil to where you think center is. Chances are, you'll just miss and get a circle (**I**). Put a dot in the middle of the circle to locate center or mark a smaller circle whose inside is merely a dot.

Laying Out Spindles

Batches of similar spindles can be laid out either on or off the lathe. Single copies or one set of legs that include a square section are most conveniently marked on a bench **(A)**. You need mark only one face for the line to be visible on the spinning wood.

In order to copy a single spindle without square sections, reduce your blank to a cylinder, then hold the spindle against the cylinder and mark the details **(B)**.

Larger numbers of identical spindles are more easily marked while spinning on the lathe using a marking batten. To make the batten, begin by drawing your pattern on a ¼-in.- (6mm-) thick piece of wood, marking the center of each groove and the sides of any bead, cove, or shoulder using a try square **(C)**. Then cut a small V-groove on the edge of the batten at each line **(D)**. Use this groove to locate a pencil point or scribe to place accurately spaced marks on a cylinder **(E)**.

A variation of the marking batten uses pins instead of grooves. Insert brad pins on the lines and snip off the heads to create a sharp point **(F)**. Then press the snipped ends against the spinning wood **(G)**.

The fewer lines you have to mark on a blank, the better. You can avoid marking with tools altogether by using the width of your various tools to gauge distances. For example, a ¾-in. (19mm) skew can be used to lay out all the detail, starting in from either end **(H)**.

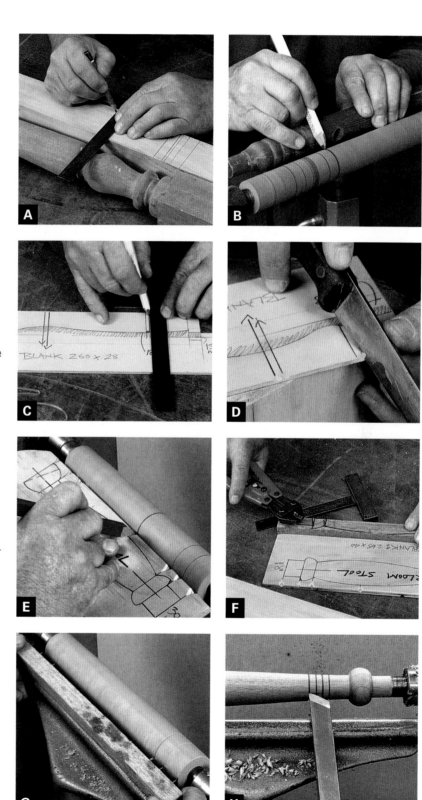

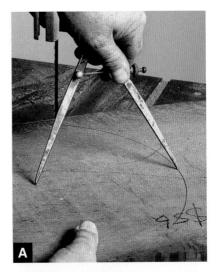

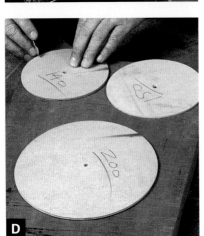

Laying Out Face Work

When laying out face-work blanks, it's best to use dividers, which scribe a line **(A)**, rather than a compass-held pencil, which wears quickly and tends to break. Marking the center hole with the point of a V-line can help you locate it later, especially if there are several holes **(B)**. When finished dimensions have to be precise, cut your discs slightly oversize and lay out the exact diameter on the lathe after the blank is turned true.

▶ See *"Turning Specific Diameters"* on p. 54.

Face-work blanks can also be laid out using a clear plastic layout template through which you can see grain patterns and defects. When the template is positioned as desired, use a spike to mark center **(C)**, then scribe the circle using dividers.

When you want to avoid puncturing an otherwise defect-free surface, use a plywood template **(D)**, or a bit of waste plywood beneath the compass point to protect the surface.

Laying Out Depth

To set a depth for hollowing, use a spurless drill. The quickest technique is to use a depth drill with the lathe running. Cut a small conical starter hole at center using a skew chisel held flat on its side **(A)**. Mark the desired depth of the hole on your drill by wrapping it with tape. I have also ground a series of marks on my drill to serve as depth indicators. Bring the drill bevel against the wood **(B)**, aligning the drill with the axis, then push it in firmly **(C)**. If the drill is correctly aligned, it will go in easily. If it isn't, it will jump around, in which case you should stop immediately and true up the starter hole.

For more accurate depth drilling, use a drill press. Set the drill press stop to retain the required thickness in the base **(D)**. For flat recesses, for example like one to be cut in a coaster, drill two holes, one at center and one farther out **(E)**.

▶ See *"Sushi Tray"* on p. 215.

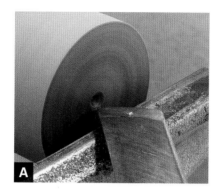

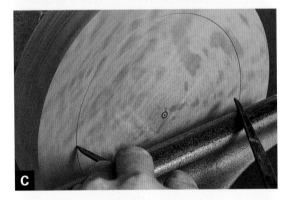

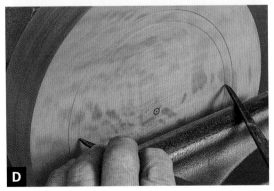

Turning Specific Diameters

Specific diameters on center work can be turned using calipers in conjunction with a parting tool. Balloon calipers set to the desired diameter are placed over the trued blank, then pulled against the wood as cutting proceeds **(A)**. When the calipers pass into space, the diameter is correct.

> ⚠️ **WARNING** Always pull spring calipers over spinning face work. Never push them.

Vernier calipers are better for gauging small diameters **(B)**. However, to prevent them from catching, the calipers' jaws must be rounded and polished (see photo on p. 48).

To mark a diameter on a face-work blank with the lathe running, begin by fixing dividers to the desired diameter. Then lay the dividers on the tool rest with the center (here marked in pencil) between the two points. Ease the left point into the wood while keeping the right point clear **(C)**. If the resulting scribed circle doesn't line up with the right point, move the left point half the distance between the right point and the circle **(D)**.

For diameters greater than the span of your dividers, use a ruler and pencil in much the same manner, marking a circle that aligns with the end of the ruler **(E, F)**. Ensure that the ruler is held level with the center.

To set the height of a center-work blank, first true the blank to a cylinder, then true the edge of the headstock face **(G)**, from which you can measure the height using a ruler and pencil **(H)**. When working repetitively, use dividers set to the required distance **(I)**.

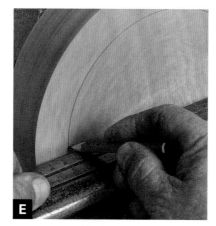

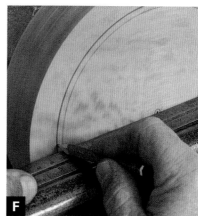

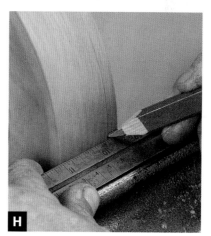

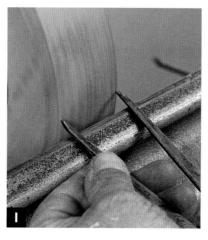

A

B

C

Measuring Depth

Whenever you start hollowing, there is a risk that you'll go too deep, so whenever possible drill a depth hole first.

➤ See *"Laying Out Depth"* on p. 53.

You can quickly gauge the depth of small-diameter projects using a pencil. With the lathe running, hold the pencil gently against the bottom of the hollow and move your thumb in line with the top of the blank **(A)**. To transfer this depth onto the profile, align your thumb with the top of the blank and touch the pencil point on the wood **(B)**.

[TIP] **When marking an internal depth on a profile in preparation for further shaping, always mark the exact depth, then work in relation to that line.**

In order to accurately gauge the depth within a wide opening, register a ruler against a straight-edge **(C)**.

Measuring Thickness

Wall thickness is most simply measured using calipers with the lathe switched off **(A)**. You'll need double-ended calipers wherever the wall thickness is less than the rim of the opening. These calipers are manufactured in a wide range of shapes designed to accommodate just about any situation. Always ensure that both jaws on a caliper meet simultaneously before you use them, and take care not to skew the jaws so you get a true measurement.

> ⚠️ **WARNING Never measure wall thickness with calipers when the lathe is running.**

When turning very thin walls on a light-colored wood, you can place a 100-watt light close behind the bowl or vase to help you gauge the wall thickness. Position the light so it won't dazzle you, then observe the amount of light coming through the wood as you make the final cuts **(B)**. Be aware that when wood is turned very thin, it tends to warp instantly. Therefore, you have time for only a couple of rapid cuts.

To measure the thickness of the base on a hollowed form while it's still on the lathe, use spring calipers with a straight arm and short finger that can reach into a chuck recess through a gap in the chuck jaws **(C)**. Adjust the caliper wheel until you feel pressure, then withdraw and close the calipers to reveal the gap **(D)**.

Alternatively, you can use rulers to measure the thickness of a base. This is easier done off the chuck and is useful for measuring rough-turned jobs about to be completed. Measure the overall height **(E)** and the inner depth **(F)**, then establish the exact thickness by subtracting the inner measurement from the outer. Don't forget to further subtract the depth of any chuck rebate or concavity in the bottom.

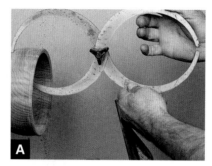

Preparing Blanks

Preparing Blanks

Converting Logs

BEFORE YOU MOUNT WOOD on a lathe, saw it as near to its final shape as possible to save both time and material. Wood that has been cut and prepared for the lathe is called a blank. Face-work blanks will be discs; spindle and end-grain blanks will be squared lengths. The grain within each blank must be aligned correctly for the object you're turning. Thus in a tool handle the grain must run the length of the blank if it's to have any strength. For much the same reason, the grain runs across the face on bowls, flat dishes, and trays.

The more symmetrical and physically balanced a blank is, the better. Unbalanced blanks vibrate, making turning difficult and often dangerous. In fact, life-threatening accidents as a result of this are not uncommon. Consequently, it is important to realize that wood varies considerably in grain density and weight, even within a single a tree. Sapwood is always lighter in weight (as well as color) than heartwood, and dense crotch wood and burls can be heavier yet. Try to use blanks that contain wood of equal density throughout.

The grain patterns in a finished object depend mostly on how the wood was cut from the tree then partly on variables like the density of growth rings, location of the pith, branches, knots, and the shape that you're turning. If you cut your blanks from commercially sawn timber, many of these decisions will have been made for you, so care is needed when selecting boards for particular patterns or grain alignment.

A portable bandsaw mill makes quick work of sawing logs into manageable sizes. The resulting slabs will be cut into a range of turning blanks.

The grain in the face-work discs (*front*), tool handle blanks (*rear right*), and end-grain blanks (*rear left*) runs from left to right.

An enjoyable aspect of turning wood is controlling the whole process, starting with a log. How you saw up a log will depend on its size, its shape, and what you want to turn. The problem is that logs are often very heavy, so you need strategies to reduce them to manageable lumps as soon as possible. Using a portable bandsaw mill is ideal but rarely practical in urban backyards where there are many trees to be had.

The good news is that short logs are most easily converted into blanks with a chainsaw. I find a 20-in. (510mm) bar quite sufficient for my bowl blanks. I cut logs into lengths that are multiples of the log diameter, adding a bit to accommodate checking at either end. Thus a 10-in.- (250mm-) diameter log is cut into lengths of about 2 ft. (600mm).

End-grain splits and checks should be eliminated from your blanks. Most logs have splits across the pith at the center as well as surface checks, which are shallow splits creeping in from the surface. Surface checks in solid or chunky forms can often be

Splits typically radiate outward from the pith. Separations between the growth rings are called *cup shakes*. Although often hard to see, they're clearly evident on the end of this board.

Most logs contain major splits across the pith at the center as well as shallow splits at the surface, called *checks*.

▶ DISTORTION

As wood dries, it shrinks in width but hardly at all in length. The outer growth rings contain the most water, so that's where the greatest shrinkage and splitting occur. Boards cut from different parts of a log distort in different ways, usually with some splitting at each end. Flatsawn boards (*A*) will cup away from center. Quartersawn boards (*B*) are the most stable, tapering only slightly while retaining flat faces. Squares (*C*) with a corner toward the pith will become diamond shaped. Splits (*D*) will develop if a log is left in the round.

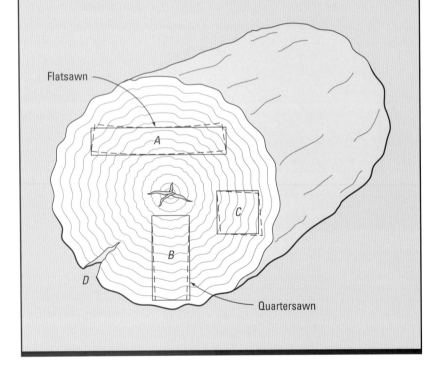

Flatsawn

A

C

B

D

Quartersawn

The shallow checks in this 5-in. (130mm) green board should be cut away when the blank is rough turned.

retained as characterful, although the checks in the 5-in.- (130mm-) thick green board shown in the photo above right would be removed when the blank is rough turned. However, you should never use blanks with splits that run right through, as the blank

will likely fly apart on the lathe, especially at high speeds. (This happens to every turner sooner or later.)

⚠ **WARNING** Any wood can fly apart when spun on a lathe, so be vigilant in checking all blanks for splits.

Before you begin sawing up logs and boards, remember that unseasoned wood will probably warp, and that you'll need to make allowances for this inevitable movement. As wood dries, it shrinks in width but hardly at all in length. And boards or blanks cut from different parts of a log will distort in different ways.

Drying and Storing Lumber

Timber needs to be seasoned (dried) so that the objects you make won't warp afterward. Wood is considered seasoned when it ceases to shrink and lose weight. Timber can season naturally over time or more quickly in kilns, but kiln-dried timber is not as nice to work as air-dried timber.

The traditional rule of thumb for air seasoning is 1 year per inch (25mm), plus a year. So theoretically, 2-in.- (50mm-) thick boards will take about 3 years to air dry. In practice, however, many timbers will dry faster, while others take considerably longer.

As wood loses moisture, splitting is almost inevitable because the outer layers shrink faster than the inner layers. The longer logs are left in the round, the more they'll split; therefore, it's best to convert them into material for blanks as soon as possible. After cutting a log into appropriate lumps and boards, coat any end grain with a wax emulsion wood sealer available from specialist woodturning stores. Small blanks can be wrapped in plastic cling (food) wrap. It's prudent to seal the entire surface of burls and areas of wild grain.

Store seasoning wood under cover, but allow air to circulate through the boards. Stack boards of manageable weight in piles separated by sawn battens, called *stickers* (see photo at top left on p. 29). Thick, heavy boards can be stood on end. A thick 6-ft.- (1830mm-) long slab is very heavy but, when standing, it is easy to "walk" it away from the pile. To cut a slab into blanks, drop it on edge onto bearers and use a chainsaw to reduce it to lumps you can lift. I try to

To minimize checking, seal the ends of logs and blanks with a wax emulsion sealer available from woodturning-supply stores.

Storing thick, heavy boards on end makes them easier to pick through and handle.

Break down a heavy slab into manageable sections by dropping it onto wooden bearers and then cutting it with a chainsaw.

prevent heavy slabs from laying horizontal because they're so difficult to move. And it doesn't get easier as you get older.

Rough Turning

For jobs that will be hollowed, you can hasten seasoning by rough turning, a process whereby you roughly shape the blank, maintaining a wall thickness equal to at least 15 percent of the diameter of the blank. A roughed job tends to warp, but not split, and stabilizes in about half the time that a solid blank will. After rough turning a blank, write the date on it so you can monitor the drying process.

To significantly reduce the drying time of green blanks, they can be rough turned and set aside to season before final turning.

Preliminary Cutting

Always start by docking (crosscutting) thin slices from each end of your log or board to get rid of splits **(A)** Examine the offcut for defects and see if it breaks. Large, thick slices should be bashed against something solid. Don't worry about small surface checks beneath the bark. Although they often run the length of the log, they will typically be cut out when the boards are sawn.

To ensure that solid wood remains, bend a thin end-grain slice to help detect any hidden splits and checks **(B)**. If there is a mass of checks, dock another chunk. However, if there is only a single split, break away any weak section on the slice and use the remainder as a pattern on the board or log, allowing you to work around the defect **(C, D)**.

On boards, cut away all heartwood splits **(E)**, then set each resulting board on its wider face. On thin boards, cut away all soft or wormy sap-wood and bark **(F)**. On thick boards in which one face is much wider than another, cut away enough bark to leave a side of clean wood at least 1 in. (25mm) wide **(G)**. From this lump **(H)**, I cut a 16-in (400mm) blank for a wide-rimmed dish. If I had cut away all the bark, the resulting board would have been only 7 in. (180mm) at its widest.

➤ See *"Bowl"* on p. 216.

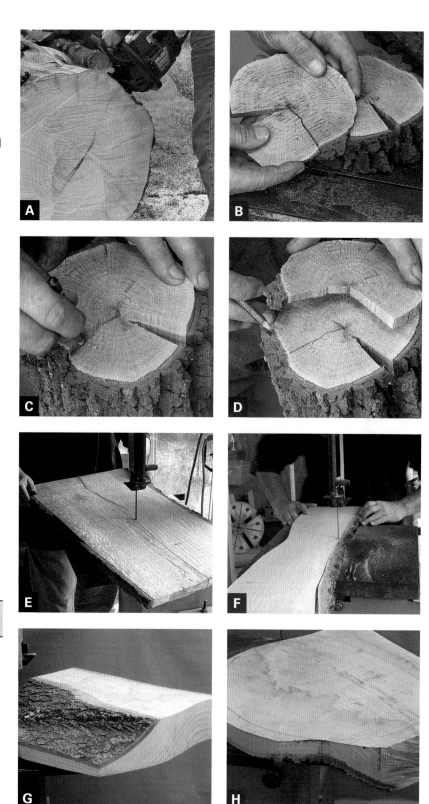

A

B

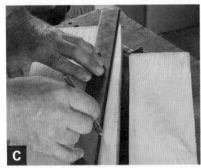

C

D

E

F

G

Blanks for Center Work

Blanks for center work such as balusters, tool handles, standard lamps, and veranda (porch) posts are square in cross section, with the grain running the length of the blank. These are most accurately sawn to size on a table saw using a fence (**A**). If the design will incorporate an unturned, square section, saw the blanks ⅛ in. (3mm) oversize, then plane them to size to remove the saw marks.

The thinner the spindle in relation to its length, the straighter the grain needs to be. Make sure the grain lies parallel to each edge of the blank. Look for straight-grained wood that is free of large knots. Be wary of fiddleback figure or wavy grain, which will break easily.

Traditionally, spindle blanks were split from small logs, then roughly shaped using an ax (**B**). Split wood is strongest because the grain runs full length through the blank. These days, however, spindle blanks are usually sawn to shape. To yield the greatest strength from a sawn blank, the grain should run parallel to its edge. If it doesn't, begin by drawing a line parallel to the grain (**C**), then cut to that line using a bandsaw. Boards too thick to cut on a table saw are sliced initially on a bandsaw (**D**). Because bandsaws are notoriously erratic, you may need to cut freehand rather than using a fence.

The ends can quickly be squared on the band-saw without using a square by sawing a shallow kerf with the board on edge, then cutting to the kerf with the board laying down (**E, F**). The resulting boards can then be cut either on a table saw, using a fence, or on a bandsaw, cutting to pencil lines (**G**).

Blanks for End Grain

Blanks for end-grain projects are simply short versions of spindle blanks. However, an end-grain blank gets mounted in a chuck. For slender objects like goblets, the grain should be straight and accurately aligned with the lathe axis for maximum strength. But for more compact or chunky boxes, paperweights, or lamp bases, the grain direction is not as crucial and you can consider using more decorative wood with twisted grain. Generally, it is best to cut away the pith because of its tendency to split. However, some slow-growing small trees and shrubs do stay intact as they season.

I make most of my end-grain blanks from offcuts and scraps, cutting on the bandsaw freehand (without a fence) for speed and convenience **(A)**. To be mounted securely in a chuck, an end-grain blank should be square in cross section, not rectangular. To prepare a blank, begin by inspecting thin crosscut slices from it, bending them to expose any defects **(B)**. If the blank is rectangular, use the narrower dimension of a slice as a gauge to lay the blank out square in cross section **(C)**. Then rip to your gauge line **(D)** to get squared lengths **(E)**.

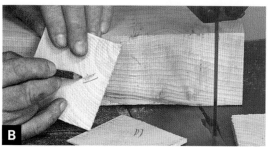

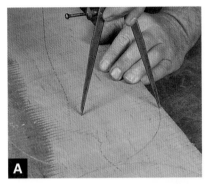

A

B

C

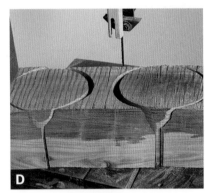

D

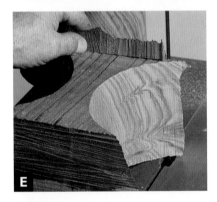

E

F

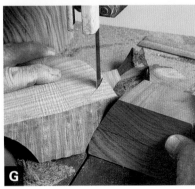

G

Blanks for Face Work

On face-work blanks, the grain runs across the face—at 90 degrees to the lathe axis. Most face-work blanks are marked out using dividers **(A)**, then cut round on a bandsaw **(B)**. On some blanks, like those for double-sided chopping boards, you don't want a compass point hole to mar the piece. In those cases, protect the face either by using a scrap of plywood beneath the compass center point or by tracing around a lay-out disc as shown in photo D on p. 52.

Wide boards are becoming increasingly scarce, but you can create a large blank by laminating together narrow, well-seasoned boards **(C)**.

Before you cut any blanks, remember that if the wood is unseasoned, you'll need to either rough turn it almost immediately or else seal the end grain to help prevent checking while the blank seasons.

➤ See *"Rough Turning"* on p. 62.

With careful cutting, you can often extract blanks from material that would otherwise be discarded. For example, this board **(D)** was not long enough to yield three discs of equal size, but there were smaller blanks to be had from the waste. I cut back the ragged corners using the first offcut to gauge how much width to retain **(E)**. Then I sawed away the center to create two blanks **(F)**. Finally, I cut the squares round using a wedge to support the undercut sides **(G)**.

> ⚠ **WARNING** When cutting blanks with undercut sides, support the overhang with a wedge.

Natural-Edge Bowls

Blanks for natural-edge bowls are cut positioning the top of the bowl toward the bark. This short half-round of timber will yield two bowl blanks. The profiles are laid out on the end grain. In a case like this, begin the layout of the first blank by positioning the ruler so the bark arches over it, then draw a line equal in length to the long-grain length of the blank **(A)**. Bisect this line at 90 degrees to establish the center of the blank (which should align roughly with the pith of the tree), then define the bottom of the blank **(B)**. Finish up by marking the sides **(C)**.

After laying out the second blank in a similar fashion, saw out the blanks clear of the lines **(D)**, and scribe the diameter on the bark **(E)**. When cutting the blanks, support any overhang with another piece of wood **(F)**.

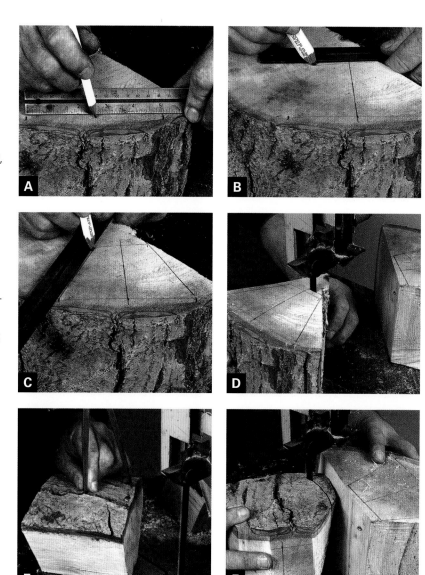

A

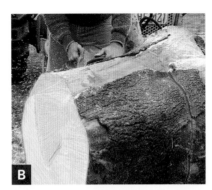
B

C

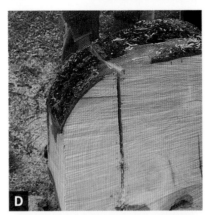
D

E

F

G

H

Slabbing Logs

Very short, thick boards suitable for bowls and hollow vessels are called *slabs*. When cutting slabs, make sure you cut clear of the pith and that your slabs don't include any heart shakes radiating from the pith.

The log shown here was cut into blanks for traditional bowls. First, a mass of end-grain checks was eliminated by cutting thick slices from the end until sound timber was reached **(A)**. Next, a length slightly longer than the log's diameter was cut to yield the bowl blanks **(B)**. After slicing away a bit of bark along one edge for stable bandsawing later, a 6-in.- (150mm-) thick slab was cut **(C)**. Because the grain needs to be symmetrical within a bowl blank due to be rough turned, a similar slab was then cut from the other side of the log **(D)**. Finally, slabs were cut from either side of center **(E, F)**.

Both larger slabs yielded four bowls **(G)**. As a bowl turner, I cut and rough turn all slabs as soon as possible after the tree is felled and before it starts to split. In contrast, I find that thinner boards destined for flat face work are best left to season whole, then cut into blanks when I'm ready to turn.

Boards can be cut accurately in almost any situation using a chainsaw mill **(H)**. Afterward, brush sawn surfaces free of dust to reduce fungal attack.

[TIP] **To spare your saw chain, use a wire brush to remove dirt and debris from grubby logs or boards before cutting.**

Converting Small Logs

I cut all logs less than 12 in. (305mm) in diameter in the workshop. I can no longer lift 4-ft.-(120cm-) long logs this diameter to the saw, so I dock lengths at floor level using an electric chainsaw **(A)**. Wedge logs in position so they don't roll and put a waste block underneath so you don't cut into the floor. The resulting rounds can then be cut on end on the bandsaw **(B)**.

To convert a small log into blanks on a bandsaw, first cut a slice off the end and mark any small splits **(C)**. Then cut a length equal to double the diameter of the slice, using a wedge to prevent the log being grabbed by the sawblade **(D)**. When a log is too long to stand on end for cutting, use wedges to prevent it from rolling as you cut lengthwise along any major split **(E)**. On this log, the left side is clear of defects and is suitable for face work. The right side is cut along the marked split **(F)** and then into squared lengths for center-work or end-grain projects **(G)**.

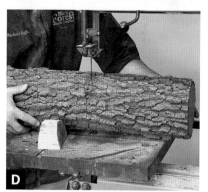

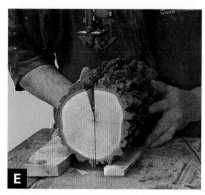

The left side is crosscut in half **(H)** in preparation for slabbing on end on the bandsaw. First, all splits are cut away from the pith face **(I)**, then a parallel face is sawn just inside the bark on the opposing edge **(J)**. When doing this, use a push stick to keep your fingers clear of the blade as it comes through the bark. Last, the disk is marked out **(K)**, then bandsawn into a circular blank.

Fixing Wood
on the Lathe

Basic Fixing

➤ Center-Work Blanks
(p. 73)

➤ End-Grain Blanks
(p. 74)

➤ Face-Work Blanks
(p. 76)

Reverse Chucking

➤ Four-Jaw Chucks
(p. 78)

➤ Jam Chucks
(p. 79)

➤ Vacuum Chucks
(p. 81)

To TURN WOOD, YOU NEED to be able to fix it securely on the lathe as quickly and easily as possible, and in a way that doesn't compromise the design of your object. There are broadly three strategies for fixing wood on a lathe. Blanks or partially completed projects can be pinned between centers, screwed to a faceplate, or held in a chuck.

Of these, mounting between centers is the simplest. Power is transmitted to the wood via prongs on a spur drive, with the opposite end of the blank supported by the tail center. This means that you cannot work all the way to center without separating the blank.

Mounting between centers is mostly for long spindles.

Faceplates are used to secure face-work blanks. Traditionally, all face-work blanks were attached to faceplates with several screws—a time-consuming process. These days, however, blanks less than 12 in. (305mm) in diameter are usually mounted on a screw chuck, which has a single, central, parallel-shank, shallow-pitch screw. Faceplates come with a lathe, whereas screw chucks don't.

In the mid-1980s, mechanical, self-centering, four-jaw chucks were developed specifically for woodturning. Chucks are

Center work, also called spindle work, is mounted between a spur drive center (*left*) and a tail center.

Face-work blanks are most easily mounted on a screw chuck on the lathe. Here a disc reduces the effective length of the screw to ½ in. (13mm).

End-grain blanks are most securely held in a chuck like this Vicmarc fitted with shark jaws. The jaws should abut a shoulder.

now regarded as essential lathe attachments for anyone turning anything other than just spindles. Each manufacturer offers a wide variety of jaws designed specifically for different jobs, but you'll probably need only two or three of these at most. You can likely manage with one or two, making other chucks yourself as the need arises. When purchasing any chuck, make sure that the thread on its adapter/insert matches the thread on your lathe spindle.

Whenever possible, chucks should grip by contracting and enclosing rather than by expanding. When you push a hollowed form over a chuck, or expand a collet within a rebate, the amount of force exerted can easily split the workpiece.

Center-Work Blanks

Blanks for center work (also called spindle work) have the grain running parallel to the lathe axis. Spindle blanks are usually mounted between centers. Locate the spur drive end first **(A)**, then fix the tail center to support the other end **(B)**. If you keep your left hand on the tool rest as you adjust the tail center, the job is a lot easier. Wind the tail center in tight, then back it off one-eighth of a turn so you support the wood without bending it.

The spur drive must bite into the wood **(C)**. On soft woods, tighten the tailstock to force the blank onto the spurs. On harder woods, tap the blank against the spur drive using a mallet **(D)** or use an old spur drive as a punch **(E)**. If you use your only spur drive for this, use a soft mallet that won't damage the end of the Morse taper. On very dense hardwoods, saw a cross at center using a carrier/jig **(F)**.

These days, it's pretty much standard to use a revolving tail center that maintains constant pressure against the wood. However, if your lathe center is solid (without a bearing), use oil to lubricate the point, then tighten the tail center **(G)**. Apply more oil and adjust the tail center whenever the job starts to rattle, squeal, or smoke. Better yet, get a revolving center.

Very slender spindle blanks are best mounted in long-nose jaws, which can grip work as small as ³⁄₁₆ in. (5mm) in diameter **(H)**. The idea is to hold the blank at the drive end and support it at the other with the tail center. Don't wind the tail center up too tight, or you'll bend the blank.

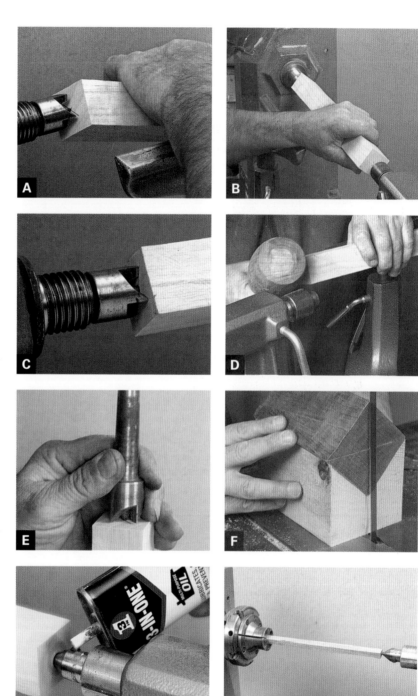

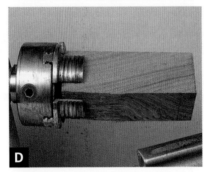

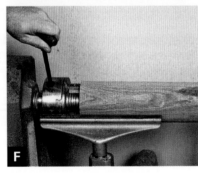

End-Grain Blanks

End-grain blanks have the grain running parallel to the lathe axis. Small, solid jobs like knobs, eggcups, and turnings that have thick bases can be mounted quickly and easily on a screw chuck. To use a screw chuck, first cut the end of a blank square to its axis, then drill a hole to accept the screw **(A)**. Mount the blank onto the chuck by winding it onto the screw **(B)** until it's snug against the face of the chuck **(C)**.

Blanks that are to be hollowed should be mounted in a chuck. Short, square blanks less than 2 in. (50mm) in diameter and 6 in (150mm) long can be mounted directly into standard jaws with few problems, although you'll waste the portion within the chuck jaws **(D)**. However because the jaws will grip a cylinder more securely, it's best to turn down the end of the blank then mount the rounded end in the chuck **(E)**. Small blanks require only a ⅜-in.- (10mm-) long tenon with a hint of a shoulder for the chuck jaws to abut. Longer tenons should be slightly shorter than the depth of the chuck jaws. Use the tail center when fitting the blank into the chuck to ensure that longer and heavier blanks sit tight against the jaws **(F)**.

Larger end-grain blanks for vases or hollow forms should be rough turned between centers and should include a short, wide tenon that will fit wide chuck jaws **(G)**.

A cup chuck is excellent for small production work, but blanks need to be cut or turned to fit. If a blank is the same diameter as the chuck, it's easy to turn a shallow taper on one end, taking the square to round and then a fraction smaller so the end just fits into the chuck **(H)**. Drive the blank into the chuck on the lathe **(I)**. To true the blank in the chuck, strike the end grain with a glancing blow **(J)**.

Smaller squares can be trimmed to size with an ax **(K)**, then driven into the chuck or even straight into a hollow drive shaft **(L)**. After the job is parted off, remove the waste from the chuck with a knockout bar as you would a spur drive.

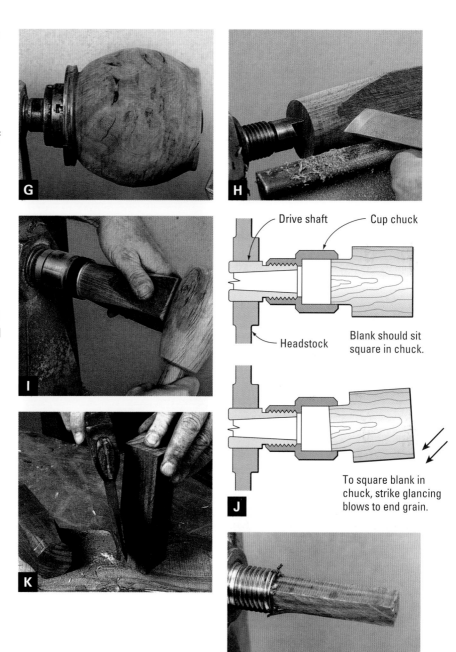

Drive shaft — Cup chuck

Headstock

Blank should sit square in chuck.

To square blank in chuck, strike glancing blows to end grain.

A

B

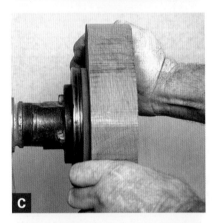

C

TIP

D

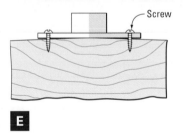

Screw

E

Face-Work Blanks

The grain on face-work blanks is aligned at 90 degrees to the lathe axis. You can use a whole range of chucking techniques for face work, including faceplates and a variety of chucks.

Faceplates are mostly used to grip a rough blank while the outside profile is being turned. After that, the job is rechucked for turning the other face or for hollowing. Occasionally, the job is then reverse chucked to remove a foot or chuck marks.

The quickest and easiest way to mount a face-work blank with a flat face is on a screw chuck. Lock the drive spindle and wind the blank on by hand. Or, if you have a variable-speed lathe, a faster alternative is to reduce the speed to about 300 rpm and offer the blank up to the screw with your palm against the face (A), pushing at first, then removing your hand as the screw bites into the wood (B). The whole operation takes less than a second. Afterward, stop the lathe, lock the spindle, and cinch the blank tight against the backing plate (C). Use as wide a faceplate as possible, because the wider the faceplate, the shorter the screw you can use. You can shorten the effective length of a screw by mounting a thin plywood or medium-density fiberboard (MDF) disc before winding on the blank (A).

[TIP] **When using a screw accessory in a chuck with standard jaws, turn a wood washer to increase the bearing surface of the chuck.**

Large blanks or those with an uneven face should be fixed to faceplate with substantial wood screws (D). Be sure to place screws either side of the axis on which the faceplate pivots (E) or use at least four screws.

Very rough lumps lacking a face that's flat enough for a faceplate, like a natural rimmed bowl, can be mounted between centers. Small blanks are most easily mounted on a two-spur drive. Using a chisel, first cut a V-groove the width of the spur drive at the center of the blank **(F)**. Locate the spur drive in the V-groove **(G)**, then tighten the tail center in position **(H)**. It's easy to realign the blank to where you want it once it's between the centers **(I)**.

Mount larger uneven blanks using a faceplate drive. Locate the faceplate in position along the top of the blank and tap the spurs into the surface **(J)**, then drill holes for the spurs **(K)**. Locate the blank on the spurs, which should fit right into the holes **(L)**, then bring in the tail center **(M)**.

> [**TIP**] To center a faceplate on a blank, scribe a circle very slightly larger than the faceplate, then set the faceplate within the circle.

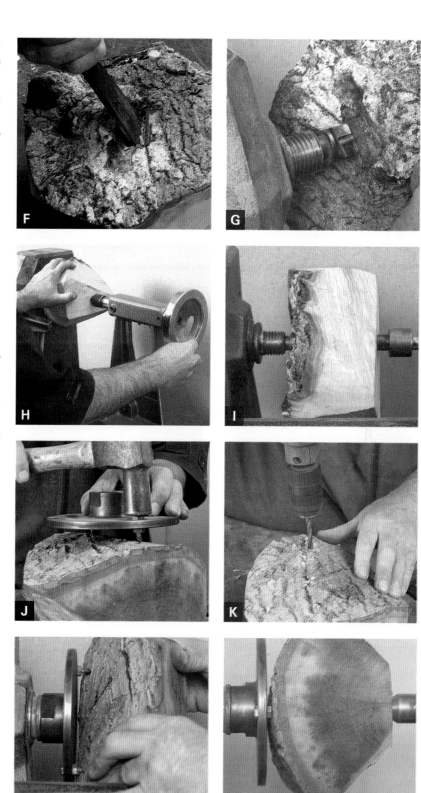

A

B

Four-Jaw Chucks

There are a number of occasions when nearly completed work needs to be reversed on the lathe to remove chuck marks or to refine a foot. Small enclosed forms can be rechucked over expanding chuck jaws **(A)**. Beware of overtightening, especially with well-used chucks whose jaws can expand slightly with centrifugal force when you start the lathe. If you hear a sharp crack as the lathe starts spinning, stop the lathe immediately and check for a split. Larger jobs can be held on bowl jaws, which include polyurethane stoppers or buttons that grasp the rim of the bowl to hold it to the chuck **(B)**. The stoppers can be relocated for gripping smaller or larger diameters or even square rims.

Jam Chucks

The simplest way to remount work for refining a foot is to use a jam chuck into or over which the job is jammed for a friction fit **(A)**. Turn these chucks as needed using various forms of scrap. Mine are made from thick medium-density fiberboard (MDF); cylinders left over from end-grain projects; defective bowls; and thick, rough-turned bowls that are still seasoning. The tapers on jam chucks should be very shallow—about 1 degree. Ideally, the rim of the object being chucked should seat against a shoulder on the chuck.

Chucks for end-grain jobs less than 3 in. (75mm) in diameter are best turned from short lengths of wood that can be held in a chuck. I hoard stubs remaining from end-grain blanks (mostly dense hardwoods) for chucks, although a softish wood like poplar is best for the job. Begin by turning a taper on the chuck that barely fits inside the opening of the job. Then, to establish the exact diameter required, hold the job just firmly enough over the taper to produce a burnish mark **(B)**. With diameters less than 2½ in. (65mm) you can do this with the lathe running. Otherwise, rotate the job back and forth on the chuck a few times to create the hint of a shiny line. Turn a very shallow taper through this mark **(C)**, then stop the lathe and ease the job onto the chuck until it's against the shoulder.

Face-work chucks

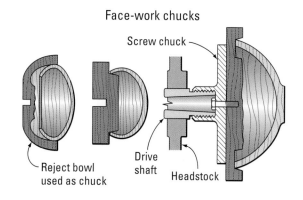

Screw chuck

Reject bowl used as chuck

Drive shaft

Headstock

Center-work chucks

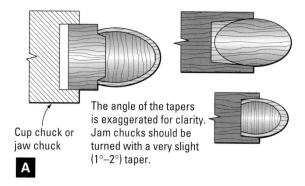

Cup chuck or jaw chuck

The angle of the tapers is exaggerated for clarity. Jam chucks should be turned with a very slight (1°–2°) taper.

A

B

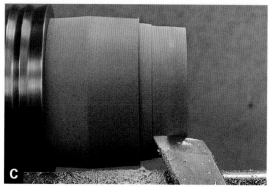

C

For larger jobs, make jam chucks from discs of thick MDF or uninspiring timber. When fitting a bowl into a chuck, turn a groove in the chuck just wide enough to contain the rim of the bowl (**D, E**). The remaining bulk can be used for chucking smaller jobs. Enclosed forms are mounted over a short tenon (**F, G**).

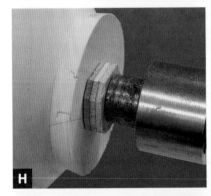

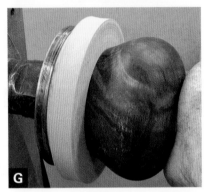

When using jam chucks, it is prudent to use tail-center support. To prevent marring the work, use a small block of MDF or plywood between the tail center and the job (**H**). (However, when you become as familiar as I am with jam chucks, chances are you usually won't bother with tail-center support, even though the slightest catch will pull the job free.) If you can't get the workpiece off the chuck, tap the chuck with a hammer, wrench, or other heavy tool to pop the job free.

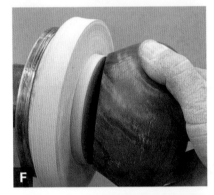

For mounting uneven edged or very thin bowls, true the edge of a disc so it fits inside the form to be mounted (**I**), then bring in tail-center support (**J**). I prevent the base from being damaged by using a flat tail center. You can purchase these, but I've turned a small block which jams over the revolving cup center.

Vacuum Chucks

Vacuum chucks allow you to reverse mount work without leaving any obvious chuck marks or fixing points. A vacuum pump is used to suck the workpiece against a chuck or faceplate **(A)**. At its simplest, an old vacuum cleaner is connected to a commercial vacuum cleaner faceplate **(B)**. To this I attached a medium-density fiberboard (MDF) disc into which is set a 6-in.- (150mm-) diameter cardboard cylinder into or over which I can mount small forms **(C, D)**. Heavy cardboard tubes can be gleaned from carpet sellers, but any heavy packing tube will do. Polyvinyl chloride (PVC) pipe is another possibility, but you'll need stretch-fabric surgical tape around both sides of the rim to create a gasket and a soft surface to prevent marring the job. Softer materials like cardboard and MDF don't usually need a gasket. However, if you have trouble getting a good vacuum seal, use the tape.

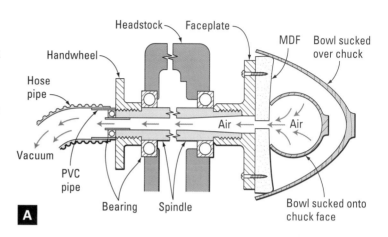

A

Sharpening

Preparation and Shaping

Sharpening

S HARP TOOLS ARE ESSENTIAL if you are
to cut wood cleanly, safely, and easily.
Turning tools remove huge amounts
of wood very quickly, and edges need constant attention if they are to remain sharp.
You can hone an edge a few times, but a
quick visit to the grinder is generally a more
effective use of time. With very abrasive
timbers, you might need to regrind every
few minutes, so sharpening is something you
want to be able to do quickly and efficiently.

If you want to use sharp tools, you must
to be able to recognize when an edge needs
sharpening. There should be no chips or
mini-bevels on an edge, and it should reflect
no light. The photo opposite left demon-
strates a variety of problems: the round-nose
scraper has a flat end that needs reshaping;
light reflecting on the edge of the disc
scraper shows that it needs honing; the
gouge edge is flat all the way and, therefore,
not sharp; and the skew edge is chipped and
the small bevels in the upper half would
make it difficult to use.

[TIP] **New gouges, chisels, and scrapers**
***always* need sharpening.**

The difference between a really sharp
edge and one less so is slight, but with practice you can feel the difference by stroking
your thumb very gently *across* the edge. If you
think an edge *might* need sharpening, it does.

Not one of these tools will cut easily. Highlights and flat sections indicate an edge that's less than sharp. Chips will also prevent an edge from cutting.

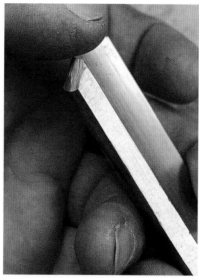

Test for a sharp edge by stroking your thumb very gently *across* the edge.

Grinding

The aim when grinding is to create a slightly concave single-facet bevel. In the photo at right the upper bevel, ground on a wet wheel, is nearly perfect. The multifaceted bevel at the center of the photo will also cut well because there are no micro-bevels on the upper part of the edge. If the tool still doesn't cut after you've ground it, look for highlights on the edge indicating flats or micro-bevels, as shown on the bottom scraper in the photo. These flats can be minuscule and still hinder cutting.

You can grind freehand or use jigs. Although jigs ensure a perfect edge, they're time-consuming to set up, and they don't always provide the best edge for a particular situation, especially on deep-fluted bowl gouges. Most professionals grind freehand, allowing them to touch-up an edge quickly as it becomes slightly dull. Freehand grinding also lets you adjust the shape for particular situations as work proceeds. That said, jigs do ensure that you get to experience a

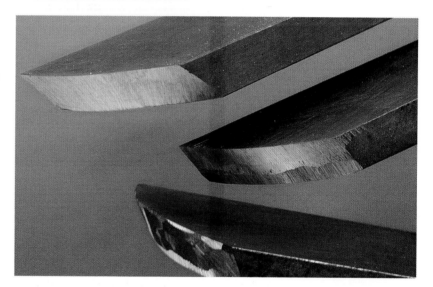

The slightly concave, single-facet bevel at the *top* is perfect. The bevel at the *center* is acceptable, but the multiple facets on the *bottom* scraper render it virtually useless.

truly sharp edge, and they help you develop a feel for the grinding procedure.

[TIP] Freehand grinding is easy if done gently and steadily. Don't push the tool too hard against the wheel, and keep HSS tools cool by dipping them in water frequently.

You can grind using either a high-speed dry wheel or a slower water wheel. A dry wheel cuts faster, but the resulting heat can burn an edge. Inexpensive high-speed grinders run at about 3450 rpm, with more costly models running around 1725 rpm. Although these slower-speed grinders are less likely to burn a tool, I prefer the faster cutting speed provided by the 3450-rpm models. When grinding a high-speed steel (HSS) tools, the trick is to keep the tool cool by dipping it in water frequently and then by not pushing the tool edge aggressively against the wheel. As the tool is ground, it should stay cool enough to hold just behind the bevel for at least 8 seconds. However, if the edge gets blue or gold with heat, a quick polish of the top of the tool should remove the discoloration. Unlike with carbon steels, accidentally burning HSS to blue won't destroy its temper.

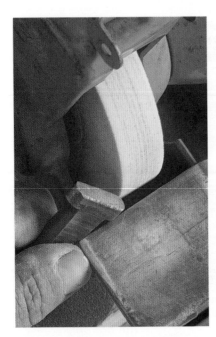

When a wheel gets grubby from metal particles, it needs cleaning. A diamond-faced dresser will easily clean and flatten the wheel at the same time.

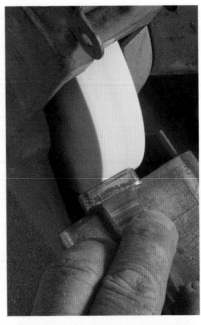

With the rest set horizontally at the center, lay the dresser flat and move it across the wheel.

Most grinders are supplied with gray vitrified wheels that clog quickly and glaze over. Although these will work, you'll get better service from white or ruby-colored friable aluminum oxide wheels or blue ceramic wheels. A 36-grit or 46-grit coarse wheel works well for rough shaping, and a finer 60-grit to 80-grit wheel is best for the final stages of grinding.

Grinding wheels must be dressed frequently so they run true, stay sharp, and remain free of the accumulated metal particles that lodge in the grit. When a wheel exhibits dark areas from the metal, clean it using a diamond-faced dresser. Hold the dresser flat on the rest while moving it across the wheel to create a flat or slightly convex surface.

Water-cooled wheels cut slowly but provide a superior edge with no risk of overheating. Therefore, it makes sense to quickly rough grind on a high-speed dry wheel and to finish a the water wheel. Regardless of the type of grinder you use, tools are held in much the same manner when sharpening.

> **WARNING** Always wear eye protection when grinding.

Preparing Tools for Grinding

The sharpest edge results from the intersection of two polished surfaces. In preparation for grinding, polish the flute of a gouge or the top of a scraper or cutter to remove any pitting or machining marks, like those on the top gouge in the top left photo opposite. You can use diamond hones or slip stones, but cloth-backed abrasives do the job simply

Pitting and machine marks like those on the gouge at the *top* hinder sharpening. A polished surface (*bottom*) will take and hold a keener edge.

Remove the marks using cloth-backed abrasive wrapped around a dowel. Avoid tipping the dowel, which will round the edge.

and inexpensively. I use 150 grit, but an ultra-smooth surface can be achieved by working through a range of successively finer grits, then finishing up with a honing compound.

The best way to polish a gouge flute is using cloth-backed abrasive held around a dowel or pencil. As you move the abrasive back and forth, be sure to keep it flat against the flute to prevent rounding over the edge.

Polish scrapers upside down against abrasive stuck to a flat surface. This should also be done to remove a burr before grinding. Keep the tool flat on the abrasive to avoid rounding over the edge. Alternatively, hone the top using a diamond hone.

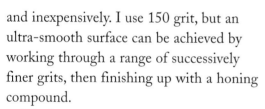

To polish the face of a scraper, rub it upside down on abrasive glued to a flat surface.

A diamond hone also works well to remove scratches and pits from the face of a scraper.

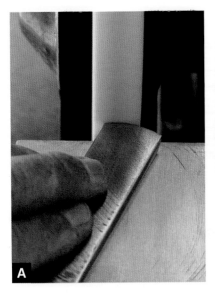

A

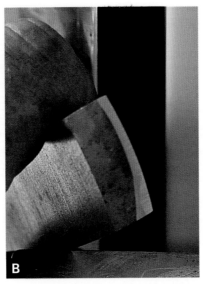

B

Shaping a Scraper Edge

Although a tool might have the cross section you need, the edge isn't always the shape required. New turning tools usually need slight reshaping, while others require major modification for specific jobs. Use a coarse 36-grit to 46-grit wheel.

To shape a scraper edge, keep the tool horizontal on the rest as you swing the handle smoothly from side to side (**A**). This creates a vertical bevel (**B**), which then needs grinding back to about 45 degrees.

➤ See *"Setting a Bevel Angle"* on facing page.

[**TIP**] **Slightly round over the edges on the underside of your scrapers so they slide more easily on the rest. Use a coarse hone or a disc or belt sander to create a small radius.**

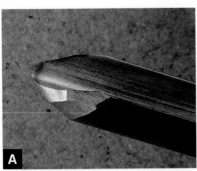

A

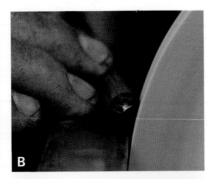

B

C

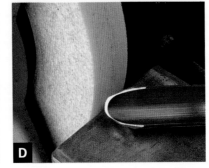

D

Shaping a Gouge Edge

To shape or restore a poorly ground fingernail gouge similar to the one shown here (**A**), set the grinder rest horizontal and commence grinding with the tool on its side. Ease the edge forward so both wings contact the grinding wheel simultaneously (**B**), then swing the handle toward you in one smooth sweep so the tool pivots onto its nose (**C**). With two light passes, you should obtain a symmetrical, rounded, convex nose with a continuous silver facet against the flute (**D**), the inside of which will be the final edge after sharpening.

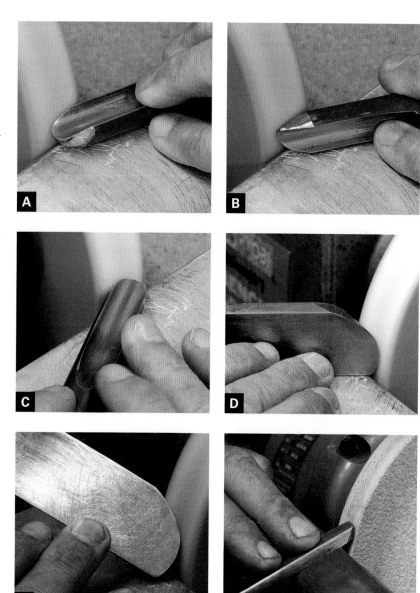

Setting a Bevel Angle

My bevels all start out at about 45 degrees. However, due to a tendency to grind less than the whole bevel, I find that they tend to become steeper than desired after repeated grindings. When this happens, I reset the bevels. The quickest way to do this is to hold the tool on its side while grinding so I can see what I'm doing.

Gouge bevels should be longer at the nose than on the wings, where they blend into the side of the blade. Begin grinding at a wing **(A)**, rolling the tool on its side to grind the nose, simultaneously pivoting the blade around so it finishes at 45 degrees to the wheel face **(B)**. To complete the process, bring the tool in from the other direction to grind the other wing in the same manner **(C)**.

Round-nose scraper bevels are shaped in the same manner, so the long bevel on a nose steepens until it melds into the vertical side. Set the bevel angle on the nose with the tool on its side **(D)**, then tilt it up to shape the bevel as it steepens toward the side **(E)**, waggling the bevel against the wheel.

You can use a waggling technique to set bevels on straight-edged scrapers. Alternatively, mark the angle on the side of the tool and use the line to set the angle of the tool rest **(F)**. Then lay the tool flat on the rest as you grind, swinging the handle slightly sideways if the edge is radiused.

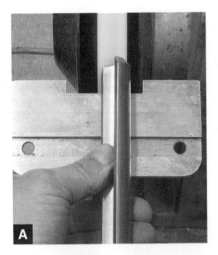

Straight and Near-Straight Edges

When grinding skew chisels, parting tools, slightly radiused scrapers, and square-ground gouges, simply keep the tool blade flat on a rest that is set at the correct angle. To maintain control, pinch the blade to the rest **(A)**. Roll the tool side to side, easing it forward into the wheel as metal is removed **(B, C)**. When sparks come over the top of the edge, you should be done. Another sign of a sharp edge when using a high-speed grinder is a slight change in the color of the metal **(D)**. On wider rests that prevent an under-hand grip, press firmly on top of the tool **(E)**.

> ⚠ **WARNING** Adjust a rest with the grinder switched off.

Some grinding systems include a platform and simple insert jigs for maintaining the skewed angle of an edge. A 90-degree jig is ideal for square-ground tools like this beading and parting tool **(F)**. For straight-edged skew chisels or scrapers, you can use an angle jig **(G)**. Manufacturers provide jigs for standard angles, but if you prefer something slightly different, it's simple enough to make your own. This jig is wood, screwed to the slider provided with the O'Donnell tool rest for the purpose. To grind a slight radius on a straight edge, swing the lower portion of the blade away from the jig as shown **(H)**. Be careful not to round over the long point on skew chisels.

On skew chisels, use a water-cooled wheel or honing stick to soften the sharp angle at the bevel heel and corners to prevent marring cleanly cut wood **(I)**.

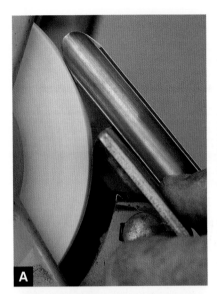

A

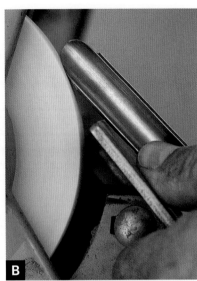

B

C

Fingernail Gouges and Round-Nose Scrapers

To get the most from a fingernail gouge or round-nose scraper, the edge should be a smooth convex curve, with a bevel steeper on the side or sides than on the nose, where 40 degrees to 45 degrees is typical. To grind this varying bevel, you need to pivot a tool on the rest freehand.

With a water-cooled stone, it's impossible to burn an edge, regardless of how forceful you are. Some water-wheel sharpening systems include jigs that make grinding gouges easy. These jigs will give you a usable edge, but they won't allow you to grind the 45-degree nose combined with short, curved, convex wings useful for turning bowls. Grinding on a water-cooled wheel is slow, so save time by rough shaping on a high-speed grinder.

To grind by hand, set the rest at a steep angle so the tool can pivot on the top edge of the rest. Start grinding with the tool on its side against the rest **(A)**. Then simultaneously raise the handle as you rotate the tool **(B, C)**, grinding to the nose, then continuing down the other wing. The same maneuver, viewed from above, shows the tool angled slightly to the left at the start **(D)**, then rolling square to the wheel with the flute up as the nose is ground **(E)**. To complete the motion, the tool angles to the right as the handle drops, and the edge is pushed upward on the wheel to grind the right wing **(F)**.

Grinding a round-nose scraper is similar to grinding a gouge **(G, H, I)**.

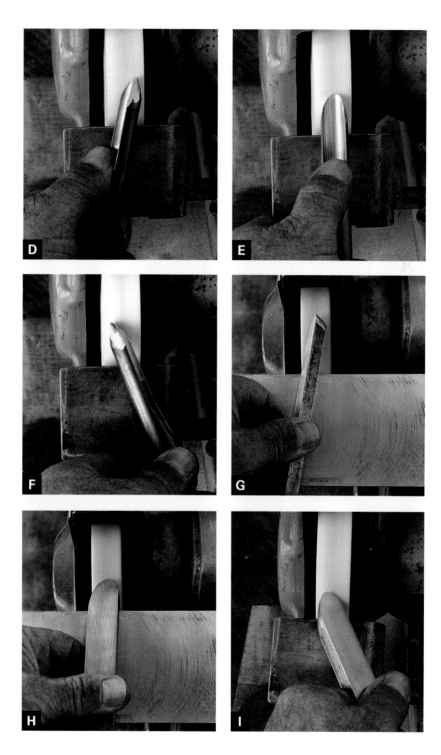

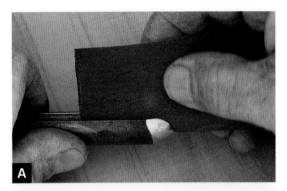

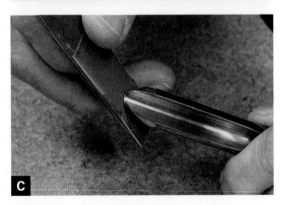

Honing

Honing is the process of bringing or restoring an edge to peak sharpness. Grinding any tool results in a *burr*—a small buildup of metal on the edge. This burr needs to be removed for a truly sharp edge. During turning, regular honing will keep the edge extra sharp.

When honing an edge, hold the tool steady against your body, a bench, or the lathe. Start by removing the burr from the top of the tool. For gouges, use 150-grit cloth-backed abrasive wrapped tightly around a dowel **(A)**. Scrub the abrasive back and forth three or four times to remove the burr. Keep it pressed firmly against the gouge flute to prevent rounding the edge.

To remove the burr from the top of a scraper, either use abrasive glued to a flat surface (see photo at middle right on p. 85) or use a diamond hone **(B)**. Both methods also work for shaped scrapers and thread chasers, on which it is not possible to hone the bevel. Take care that the hone maintains contact with the tool face at all times to prevent rounding over the teeth or edges.

After removing the burr, hone the bevel **(C)**, ensuring that the hone stays in constant contact with the bevel heel so you don't round over the edge.

Hook Tools

There is still a lot of interest in hook tools, although for many jobs these have been superseded by longer-lasting scrapers and gouges. To sharpen a hook tool, begin by grinding the outside, using a wet stone to prevent burning the edge. Press the tool firmly against the rest initially **(A)**, then against your thumb as you complete the upward motion **(B)**. In this case, rotate the wheel away from the edge (clockwise in the photos).

I grind the inside of this André Martel hook tool using a low-speed grinding cone mounted in a drill press. A diamond cone is best. When doing this, steady your hand on the drill press table so you can precisely manipulate the edge against the stone **(C)**. Thereafter, keep the edge keen by honing the inner edge with small round diamond stick **(D)**.

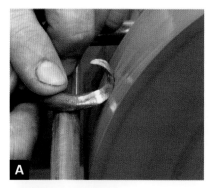
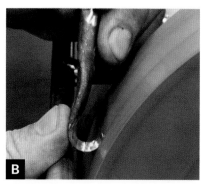

Cutters

The flat cutters typically found on deep-hollowing tools and shear scrapers are difficult to grind freehand, especially on a high-speed grinder (although you can hold them in pliers to prevent burning your fingers.) It's better to use a grinding jig on a water-cooled wheel to eliminate any possibility of burning the edge **(A, B)**. When you need to hone a cutter during grinding, don't remove it from the jig or you'll lose your setting **(C)**.

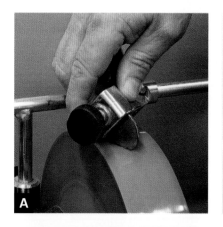
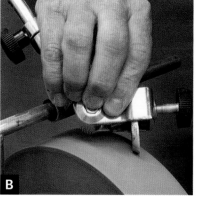
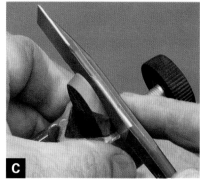

Spindle Techniques, page 96

Spindle Projects, page 108

PART THREE

Spindle Work

SPINDLE TURNING IS THE BACKBONE of the craft of turning wood on a lathe. For many centuries, woodturners used lathes to mass produce by hand millions and millions of round components for the furniture and building trades, as well as items for everyday use. The bulk of these components—ranging from camel nose pins to baseball bats to chair legs—have been some form of spindle, with the grain running the length of the object and parallel to the lathe axis. Also called center work, spindle work is turned mostly between centers, although some short objects like knobs are held in a chuck.

Spindles are like music in that a limited number of components—beads, coves, and fillets—can be combined like notes to create a nearly infinite number of variations on basic themes. These components will differ in diameter and length and will be used in a range of mixtures to create unique pieces.

Spindle Techniques

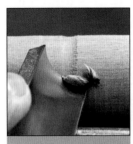

General Approach

➤ Roughing to Round (p. 100)

Spindle Detailing

➤ V-Grooves (p. 101)
➤ Beads (p. 102)
➤ Narrow Beads (p. 104)
➤ Coves (p. 105)
➤ Ogees (p. 106)
➤ Pommels (p. 107)

I N THIS SECTION, YOU'LL LEARN how to turn spindles. We'll cover basic tool-handling principals, how to avoid catches, and how to transform a rough blank into a cylinder. Then you'll see how to turn the basic decorative elements: beads, coves, grooves, and ogees. These elements are found the world over on chair and table legs, balusters, veranda (porch) and newel posts, and other long thin turnings.

For a turner, the main benefit of smothering a spindle in decorative detail—or merely tapering it slightly—is that the cuts are across the grain and, therefore, always clean, whereas on a cylinder the grain often picks out. This is why traditional spindles, typically consisting of a collection of curves decorated with grooves, are mostly devoid of cylindrical sections.

Center-Work Tools

Tools used for center work include roughing gouges, skew chisels, shallow gouges, and parting tools. The size of the tools used depends partly on the scale of the spindle and partly on personal preference. Small tools are employed only for small work, whereas larger tools can be used on both small and large diameters, although not so conveniently on thin spindles and small detail. You need only one roughing gouge, and it can be either deep or shallow.

Center-work tools (*from top*): detail gouge, skew chisels, beading and parting tool, shallow and deep roughing gouges.

The skew chisel is the main tool used for center work. Although the skew chisel has a fearsome reputation for catching, the truth is that catches with bowl gouges can be far more dramatic and dangerous. Skew catches are merely irritating and frustrating by comparison, so don't be put off. The skew is a wonderful tool and fun to use once you get the hang of it.

I use a ³/₄-in.- (19mm-) wide skew chisel for just about every spindle up to 3 in. (75mm) in diameter. For larger-diameter jobs, I prefer the stability and strength of a heavier ³/₈-in.- (9mm-) thick, 1¹/₂-in.- (40mm-) wide skew I adapted from a scraper. To make a skew slide easily along a rest, sand or hone the sharp angles on the sides to a small radius.

Most detail work is done with a ¹/₂-in. (13mm) detail gouge, although a ³/₈-in. (9mm) tool is easier on spindles less than 1¹/₄ in. (30mm) in diameter.

General Approach to Cutting

It is possible to slice the wood so cleanly that hardly any sanding is required. The constant in woodturning is the wood spinning down onto the tool edge. If the cutting portion of the edge lies at about 45 degrees to the oncoming wood, it slices the wood cleanly. Whenever you are turning, try to keep 45 degrees in mind. As an edge lies steeper to the oncoming wood, the shavings narrow until a vertical edge won't cut at all. The nearer an edge lies to horizontal, the wider the shaving and the greater the risk of a heavy catch. A horizontal edge used at 90 degrees to the job will scrape, leaving an inferior surface.

The key to controlled turning is to let the wood come to the tool. That is, don't push the edge into the spinning wood; think of holding the edge at the most favorable angle (about 45 degrees) so the wood is sliced as it comes down onto the edge. As wood is removed, the tool is eased forward. As cutting proceeds, gouge and skew chisel bevels should contact the wood but not be pressed against it. All center-work cuts go from larger

With any tool, the cleanest shearing cut results from an edge held at 45 degrees to the oncoming wood.

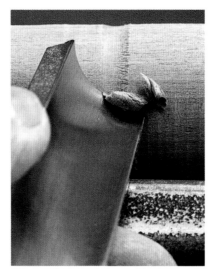

to smaller diameters, as indicated by the arrows in the drawing below.

To become familiar with the essential center-work cuts, practice on 2-in. to 2½-in. (50mm to 65mm) squares about 10 in. (250mm) long. A blank that is no longer than your tool rest will save you the trouble of adjusting the rest. Set the tool rest so that you can hold tools comfortably. Assuming the lathe center is about elbow height, the rest should initially be set just above center, then dropped as the diameter decreases. If you are short and working at a relatively high lathe, the rest should be set low; if you are tall and working at a low lathe, it should be set high.

Catches and Chatter

Catches and chatter marks spiraling around a spindle can be frightening and frustrating. Both can be avoided. A *catch,* when the tool is grabbed by the wood and smacked down onto the rest, occurs whenever the wood

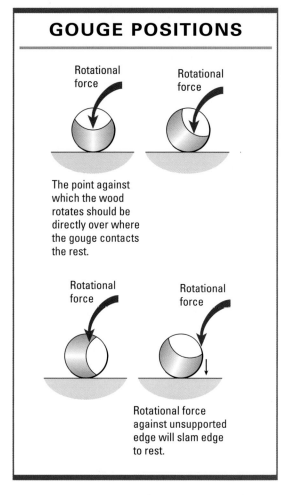

GOUGE POSITIONS

Rotational force

Rotational force

The point against which the wood rotates should be directly over where the gouge contacts the rest.

Rotational force

Rotational force

Rotational force against unsupported edge will slam edge to rest.

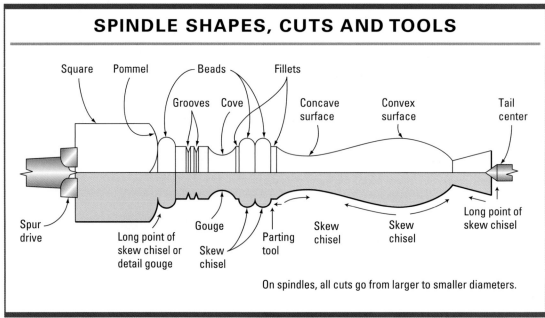

SPINDLE SHAPES, CUTS AND TOOLS

Square   Pommel   Beads   Fillets

Grooves   Cove

Concave surface   Convex surface   Tail center

Spur drive

Long point of skew chisel or detail gouge

Gouge

Skew chisel

Parting tool

Skew chisel

Skew chisel

Long point of skew chisel

On spindles, all cuts go from larger to smaller diameters.

Lathe Speeds for Even-Grained Center-Work Blanks

Speeds shown in revolutions per minute (rpm). Blanks with uneven grain and density should be started at half the stated speed, then increased as the balance of the blank allows.

DIAMETERS	6"(150mm)	13"(305mm)	18"(460mm)	24"(610mm)	36"(915mm)	48"(1220mm)
½"(13mm)	2500	2100	1500	900	—	—
2"(50mm)	2000	2000	2000	1500	1200	1000
3"(75mm)	1500	1500	1500	1500	1200	1200
4"(100mm)	1000	1000	900	800	700	700
5"(125mm)	900	900	700	700	600	600
6"(150mm)	500	500	500	500	400	400

rotates against an unsupported tool edge. The simplest catch happens when you put the tool edge to the wood before laying the blade on the rest. All other catches are a variation of this. A shallow gouge will catch if you use it flute up while trying to cut with the side, as shown in the drawing at right. Avoid skew chisel catches by cutting with the leading lower half of the edge.

Chatter marks develop because the wood bounces against the tool and vice versa. To prevent chatter, the wood needs to run true on its axis as you cut it. To avoid the bouncing, don't push the tool hard against the wood as you cut. And when turning thin stock, support the wood using your hand or a steady (see photos on p. 14).

▶ See *"Long Thin Spindles"* on p. 119.

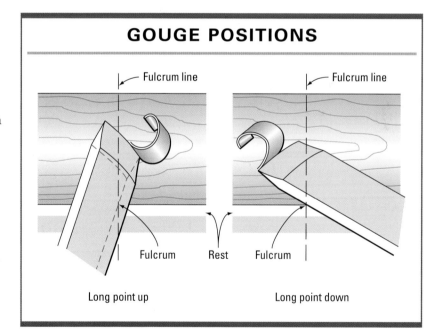

GOUGE POSITIONS

Fulcrum line

Fulcrum line

Fulcrum   Rest   Fulcrum

Long point up   Long point down

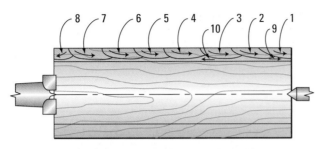

Cuts 1–8: Remove square corners with roughing gouge
Cuts 9–10: Smooth blank with skew chisel.

A

Roughing to Round

Before receiving any detailed shaping, squared blanks need to be reduced to a cylinder. Use either a deep-fluted or shallow 1-in. (25mm) roughing gouge to take a series of scooping cuts starting at the tailstock end **(A)**. The idea is to reduce the square to almost round as quickly as possible while retaining a vestige of the original square. Keep the gouge rolled in the direction you are cutting, using an overhand grip to deflect the shavings from your face **(B)**. At the other end, roll the tool to cut in the opposite direction off the end of the blank **(C)**. Don't remove more wood than is necessary.

With the corners removed, take a couple of cuts the length of the cylinder to remove any undulations **(D)**. This leaves you with a broad spiral running the length of the cylinder, which needs to be smoothed with a skew chisel. First use the chisel long point up to take a cut, moving off the right end **(E)**. Then flip the tool over to cut to the opposite end. Have the tool pointing in the direction you're cutting, with the long point down **(F)**. You can use the skew with the long point up or down, but it's less likely to catch with it down.

Blanks less than 1 in. (25mm) square can be roughed using only a skew chisel, again working back from one end. To avoid cutting into the spur drive, cut across the grain about ⅜ in. (9mm) from the end **(G)**, then cut up to that point **(H)**. You can also use the skew long point up to smooth the cylinder **(I)**.

B

C

D

E

F

G

H

I

V-Grooves

V-grooves should be cut using the skew chisel long point down. For deep grooves, pivot the skew point through an arc into the wood before easing it forward **(A)**. Start by marking center **(B)**, then make subsequent cuts in from either side using the long point of the skew **(C, D)**. The key to cutting a groove without catching the tool is to align the bevel in the direction you want to cut, then ensure that the side of the bevel maintains contact with the surface just cut. Note that the edge is clear of the wood and that the cut is made with the point.

For practice, cut a set of grooves ⅜ in. (9mm) deep and about 1¼ in. (30mm) apart. Try to get them symmetrical.

Grooves can be cut with less risk of a catch by using a detail gouge with a long bevel and fingernail grind. The disadvantage of using this tool is that the thickness and shape of the gouge prevent you from cutting deep and narrow grooves. As with the skew chisel, line up the bevel in the direction you want to cut and start by pivoting the edge into the wood **(E)**. At the bottom of the groove, roll the gouge on its side so it doesn't catch the other side of the groove **(F)**.

Arc the point into the wood (A), then push the point toward the center (B). Mark the center of the V (cut 1), then cut in from either side (cuts 2–6).

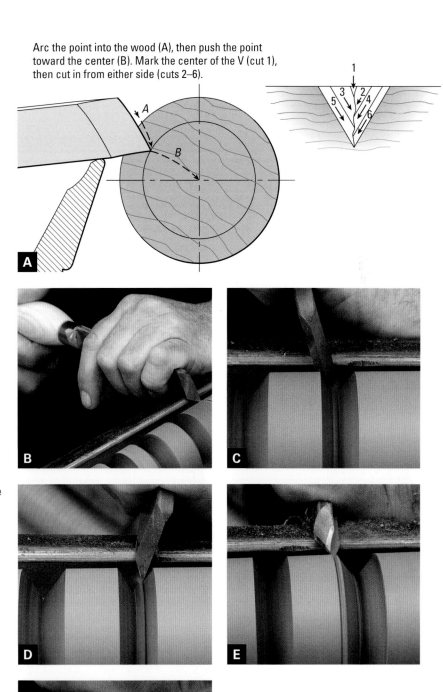

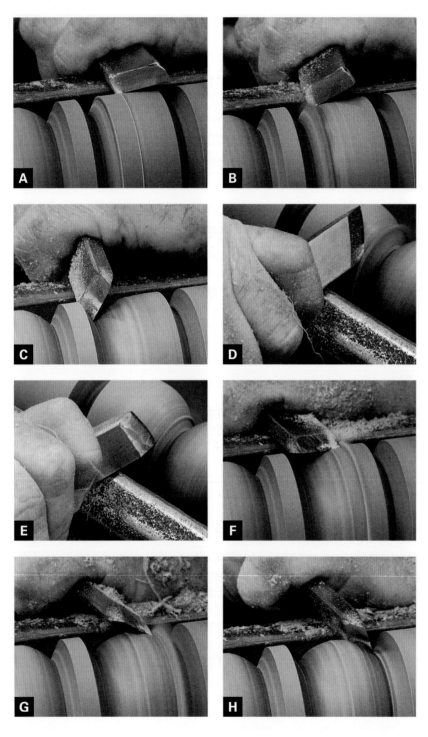

Beads

Turning a bead successfully is one of the true joys of woodturning. When turning beads, use the corner of a sharp chisel and let the wood come to the tool rather than pushing the tool hard into the cut. Also, err on the side of caution, taking a series of smaller cuts rather than one big one.

Initially define the width of the bead with a pair of grooves. Start cutting at the center of the rough bead with the skew bevel riding the wood **(A)**, then roll the tool slightly as you push it along the rest **(B, C)**. The trick is to move the tool smoothly without forcing the edge into the wood. Beads can be cut in a couple of passes, but it's best to initially take very light cuts as you develop the curve. What you cut away cannot be replaced, so proceed cautiously.

As the curve becomes steeper **(D)**, you lose sight of the corner as it cuts. To better see what's happening, remove the tool, then bring it back long point down to finish the cut **(E)**. Now mirror these cuts to form the other side of the bead **(F, G, H)**. Note that the edge is clear of the bead as the corner cuts.

A favorite professional tool for turning beads is a ½-in. (13mm) square-sectioned, square-ground beading and parting tool. It's used almost the same way as a skew chisel, but angled slightly toward the cut **(I, J)**. Using a beading and parting tool like this allows you to cut more efficiently because you don't need to flick the tool over as you cut one direction, then another.

Beads can also be cut using a detail gouge with a long fingernail-ground edge. However, as when cutting a groove, a gouge will not fit into as narrow a space as a skew chisel, preventing you from detailing the join where a pair of fully rounded beads meet.

Start the cut on top of the roughed bead with the bevel rubbing **(K)**, then roll the tool slightly as you ease it along the rest **(L)**. At the end of the cut, the gouge needs to be on its side with the nose detailing the join at the base of the curve **(M)**. Mirror these cuts to turn the other side, making sure you cut with the lower nose of the tool **(N, O)**.

To practice beads, cut a series of evenly spaced V-grooves, then round over the cylindrical portions in between using the corner of either a skew chisel or a beading tool **(P)**. A gouge is less satisfactory. While you're learning, it can help to mark the center of each bead with pencil.

➤ See *"V-Grooves"* on p. 101.

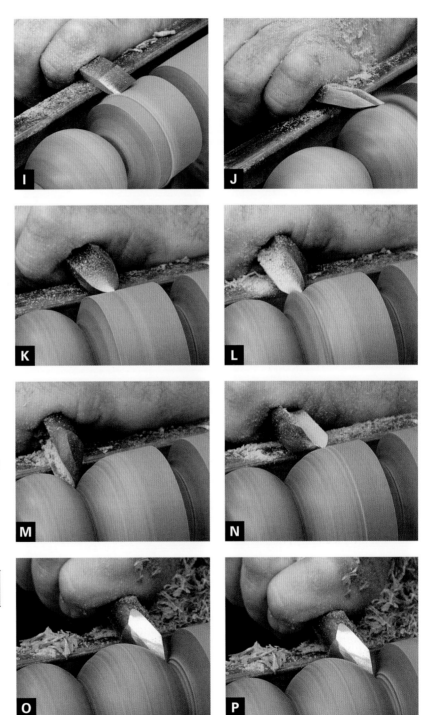

Narrow Beads

Because narrow beads are difficult to roll, they are first blocked out, then peeled into shape. This ³⁄₁₆-in.- (5mm) wide bead is turned using a ³⁄₄-in. (19mm) skew chisel.

Define the width of the bead with the skew's long point **(A)**. Next, make V-cuts using the skew chisel's long point to block out the bead **(B, C)**. Finally, use very delicate peeling cuts to round over the chamfers **(D, E)**.

Coves

Coves are best cut using a detail gouge, but a standard shallow gouge will work on diameters up to 3 in. (75mm), after which the strength of a thicker detail gouge is preferable. Cuts are made from either side **(A)**.

Mark the width of the cove, then take a couple of roughing cuts inside the lines **(B)**. Next, line the bevel up with the direction you want to cut, and pivot the edge into the wood **(C)**. To avoid a catch, the gouge must be kept on its side with the flute facing into the cove. As you cut toward the center, roll the tool but keep the cut just below the nose of the gouge, where you see shavings in the photo **(D)**.

Mirror these cuts on the other side **(E, F)**, and finish up by removing any ridges with the nose of the tool **(G)**.

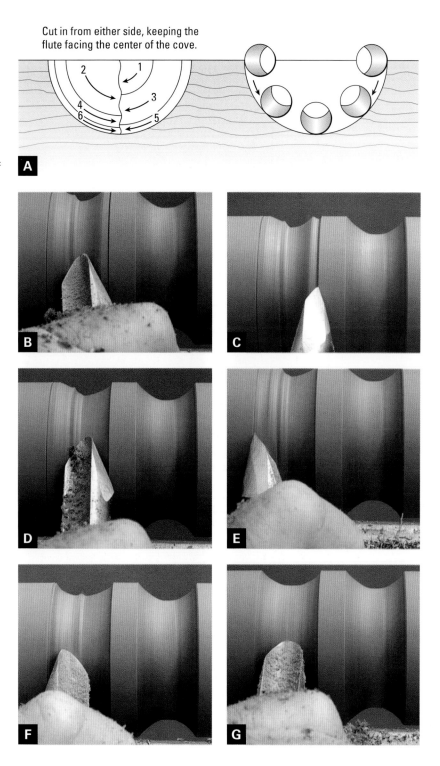

Cut in from either side, keeping the flute facing the center of the cove.

Ogees

An ogee is an S-shaped combination of cove and bead commonly used on decorative spindles. It is best cut with a gouge.

The upper portion is a cove, so start the gouge on its side **(A)**. Once the bevel is rubbing, gradually rotate the tool **(B)**, following the curve of the ogee. As the cut proceeds around the convex curve, roll the tool on its side again so the point can define the end of the curve **(C)**.

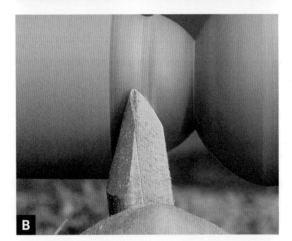

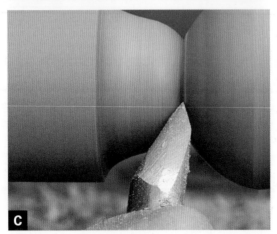

Pommels

The transition from a square section to a round on a spindle is called a pommel. Many table and chair legs and newel posts include square sections with pommels. The techniques used for cutting a pommel are the same as those used to cut grooves, coves, and ogees, although there is limited wood for the bevel to rub against. The trick is to move the tool steadfastly on its path, regardless of whether it's contacting wood or hanging in open space. That way, the bevel contacts the pommel shoulder as it passes. If you push the tool too quickly against the wood, it will slip into a gap and get caught on the next descending shoulder.

Mark the square section with a single line on the square blank. Use the long point of the skew chisel to cut a V-groove near the line, which is clearly seen on the spinning wood **(A)**. Continue to deepen the V, keeping the pommel side steep until the bottom is almost solid wood, then take a single cut on the pommel line to create a clean surface **(B)**.

To create the cylindrical section, you can use a roughing gouge to remove the bulk of the waste, although I prefer a skew chisel on diameters up to 2 in. (50mm) **(C)**. Drop the tool handle slightly so you cut into the intersection with the short corner of the skew to leave a well-defined corner **(D, E)**.

A pommel can be rounded using the long point of a skew chisel **(F)**. Clean up any lifted grain at the intersection by cutting a small V-groove, moving into the cut from the right with a minuscule downward arcing motion **(G)**. This results in a very neat transition **(H)**.

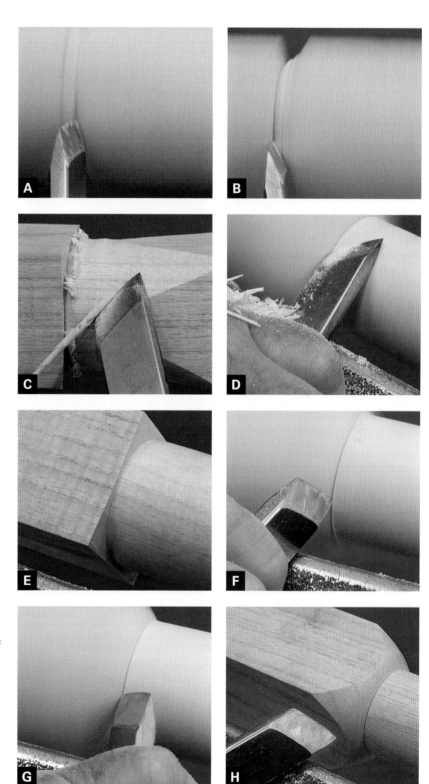

Spindle Projects

Handles

Legs

Sundry

WHEN MAKING THE SPINDLE projects in this section, you'll apply all the techniques covered in Section 10. This selection of procedures will help you develop turning skills useful when working on a range of similar projects.

The instruction on making tool handles will serve you whether you're turning full-size handles for your turning tools or a tiny gouge like the one shown in the photo at right. The table leg with pommel shows how to proceed when turning a spindle of any scale, even a much larger architectural veranda (porch) or newel post. The cabriole leg project is fun, challenging, and great practice for offset turning. The description of split turning shows you how to create beautiful applied elements for furniture and architectural woodworking. And the discussion on turning long thin spindles will prepare you for making slender items like pens and lace bobbins.

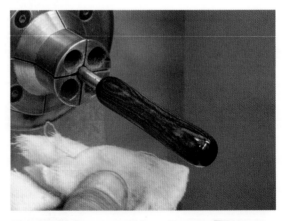

The blank for a small handle can be glued to a tool before it's turned. Long jaws grip the tool while the blank is shaped.

Small Tool Handle

For small tool handles that don't require a ferrule, select a dense hardwood like this cocobolo and use a drill press to bore a hole in the blank the size of the tool shaft **(A)**. Glue the tool into the handle with cyanoacrylate adhesive and fix the job on the lathe with the tool shaft in a chuck and the handle blank clear of the jaws. Although tail-center support is not essential, it's a good safety measure as turning proceeds **(B)**. Before sanding, turn the end using the skew chisel's long point **(C)**. All that's left is to apply a finish **(D)**.

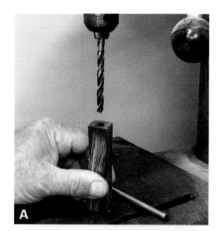

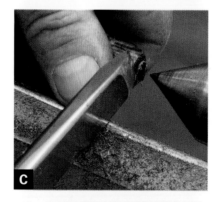

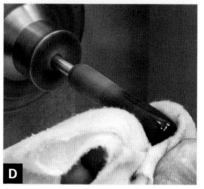

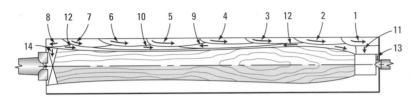

Cuts 1–10: Roughing cuts with roughing gouge
Cut 11: Size tenon for ferrule using parting tool.
Cut 12: Finish shaping using skew chisel.
Cut 13: Trim end grain flush with ferrule using long point of skew chisel.
Cut 14: Part off using long point of skew chisel.

A

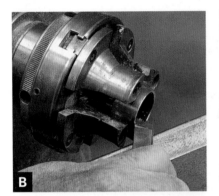

B

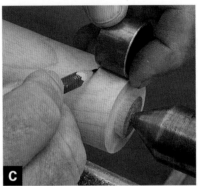

C

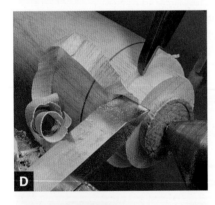

D

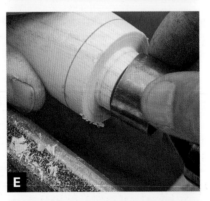

E

F

G

Tool Handle

The length of your handle should suit the tool it's for **(A)**. This turning-tool handle is made from a straight-grained ash blank about 15 in. (380mm) long and 1⅜ in. (35mm) square, with no knots or hint of cross-grain. The handle needs a ferrule ¾ in. to 1 in. (19mm to 25mm) in diameter, which you can make from scrap copper plumbing pipe.

[**TIP**] **Varying the shape and details on your turning-tool handles will help you identify your tools, even when they're half buried in shavings.**

To make a ferrule, mount a short length of the pipe in long-nose jaws and turn each end true by scraping. Then round over the edges—particularly the inner lip—so it doesn't catch the end grain when the ferrule is driven onto the handle later. Run the lathe at about 400 rpm, using a skew chisel or the bevel side of a high-speed steel (HSS) scraper to do the rounding **(B)**.

Rough the square blank to a cylinder and mark the length of the ferrule on the tailstock end **(C)**. Set your calipers to the inside diameter of the ferrule and turn the end to accept the ferrule, using the calipers (Vernier calipers are shown) to determine the correct diameter **(D)**. Use a beading and parting tool or a skew chisel laid flat on the rest for a peeling cut.

The ferrule should fit tightly enough that it will need to be driven on. To achieve the best fit, turn part of the tenon close to its final size, then chamfer its end and test-fit the ferrule on it **(E)**. The line where the ferrule rubs indicates the exact diameter required. Complete the tenon, then ease the long point of the skew chisel about ⅟₆₄ in. (0.5mm) into the corner to cut across the outer layer of fibers **(F)**. That way, if the fibers are sheared away as the ferrule is driven on, they will break cleanly away from the tenon shoulder. After turning the tenon, drive the ferrule against the shoulder using a similar ferrule **(G)**.

After fitting the ferrule, remount the blank and complete the turning. First cut the tenon flush to the end of the ferrule using the skew chisel's long point **(H)**. If you need to remove a lot of waste, you might have to tighten the tail center.

Next, roughly shape the handle using a gouge, but complete the turning with a skew chisel for the smoothest surface **(I)**. As the handle gets thinner you'll probably need to support the back of the cut with your hand to eliminate chatter marks **(J)**. Sand the handle and ferrule and apply a wax finish. Complete the turning by cutting a deep V near the spur drive, then part off with the skew chisel's long point **(K, L)**.

Finally, bore the tang hole in the handle using a drill mounted in a chuck on the lathe. The conical hole left by the tail center makes centering the handle against the drill tip easy **(M)**. At the opposite end, remove the tail center and seat the butt of the handle directly against the tail shaft **(N)**. Grip the handle firmly, switch on the lathe, and wind in the tail center to force the handle onto the drill **(O)**. The butt can then be sanded by hand or by rotating it against a small sanding disc mounted in the lathe chuck.

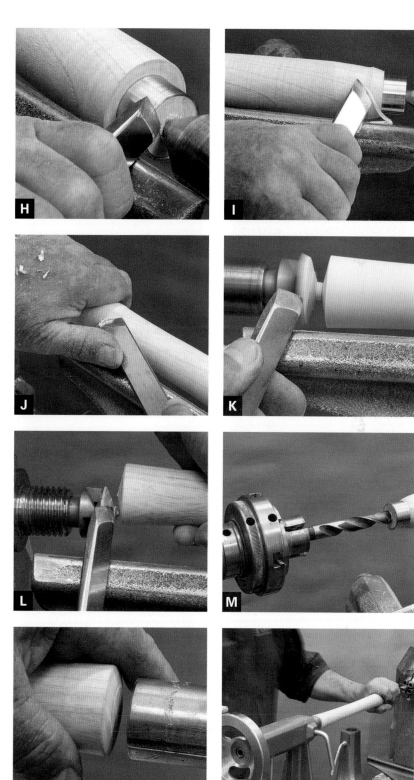

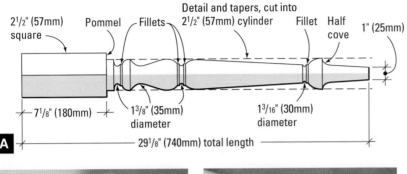

2¹/₂" (57mm) square — Pommel — Fillets — Detail and tapers, cut into 2¹/₂" (57mm) cylinder — Fillet — Half cove — 1" (25mm)

7¹/₈" (180mm)

1³/₈" (35mm) diameter

1³/₁₆" (30mm) diameter

29¹/₈" (740mm) total length

A

Table Leg with Pommel

Fix the blank accurately between centers, bearing in mind that accurate mounting is essential if the cylindrical section is to lie symmetrically within the square of the pommel **(A)**. Mark out the end of the pommel on the dressed blank and cut a V-groove to that line using the long point of the skew chisel **(B)**. Next, turn the cylindrical section using a roughing gouge **(C)**. Then lay out the detail using a story stick **(D)**.

▶ See *"Laying Out Spindles"* on p. 51.

Cut in the fillets with a parting tool, using calipers to gauge the correct diameters **(E)**. To shape the combination of coves, fillets, and half beads, use a detail gouge with a fingernail grind to cut coves **(F)** and a skew chisel for the convex shapes **(G)**.

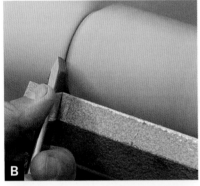

B

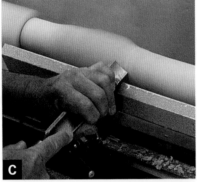

C

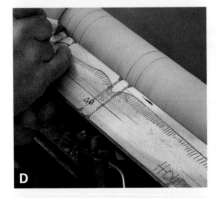

D

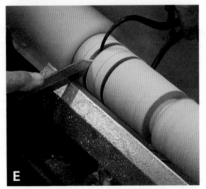

E

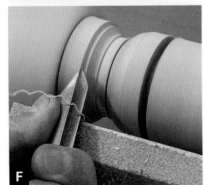

F

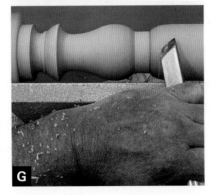

G

To avoid changing tools, use the gouge to cut both the cove and its associated fillets **(H, I)**. Take care to roll the gouge on its side to create sharp intersections.

To shape the long taper, remove the bulk of the waste with a roughing gouge, then smooth the surface with a skew **(J)**. While the skew is in your hand, use it flat on the rest to peel away the waste at the bottom of the leg **(K)**, then cut the half bead to the left **(L)**.

Turn the cove and fillet using the detail gouge **(M)**. Then cut the half cove **(N)**, taking it far enough down the leg that the skew can begin to complete the job without scoring the curve **(O)**. After sanding the turning, you should end up with a surface and detail that look something like that shown here **(P)**.

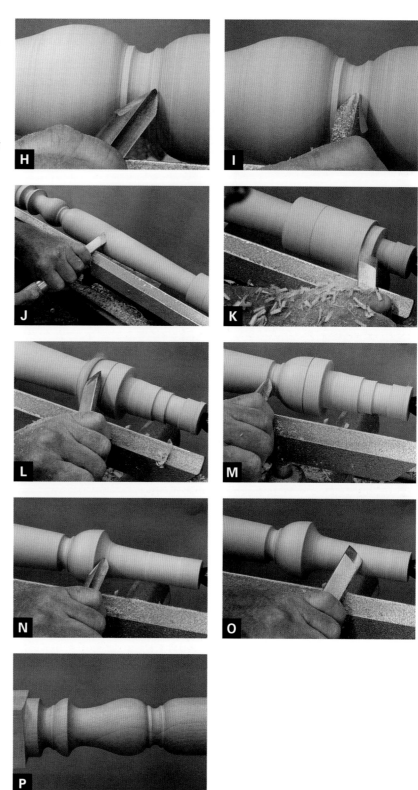

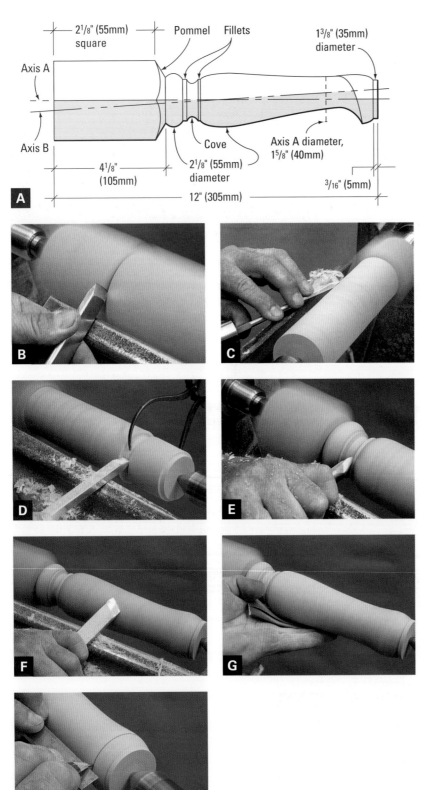

Axis A

2¹⁄₈" (55mm) square

Pommel Fillets

1³⁄₈" (35mm) diameter

Axis B

4¹⁄₈" (105mm)

Cove

2¹⁄₈" (55mm) diameter

Axis A diameter, 1⁵⁄₈" (40mm)

³⁄₁₆" (5mm)

12" (305mm)

A

B

C

D

E

F

G

H

Cabriole Leg

Cut the blank and lay out the position of the pommel **(A)**. The blank should be ³⁄₁₆ in. (5mm) longer than the final leg so that the sole of the foot can be finished without leaving chuck marks.

Begin by cutting the pommel shoulder using the skew chisel's long point **(B)**. Then turn the lower portion of the leg to a cylinder, initially using a roughing gouge, then smoothing the surface with a skew chisel **(C)**.

Next, cut in the diameter of the foot and the narrowest part of the leg **(D)**, then size the fillets and use a detail gouge to turn the associated bead and cove **(E)**.

Turn the leg, leaving a ³⁄₁₆-in.- (5mm-) long cylinder of waste at the foot **(F)**. Then sand the entire leg **(G)** before marking the location of the toe **(H)**.

Reposition the blank to axis B **(I)**. This typically is about one-third of the diameter from the rim. On the new axis, use a detail gouge to cut the curve of the foot, beginning at the left side of the blurred line. Continue until the double image nearly disappears **(J)**. Now complete the leg using a skew chisel **(K)**, eliminating the double image from the knee to the ankle. At this point, sand from the knee to the ankle with the piece spinning on the lathe **(L)**.

After sanding, remount the leg on the original axis A. Sand away the pencil mark on the foot, and turn away the waste to remove the axis B center mark **(M)**. Part off as far as you can **(N)**, then pare away the remainder with a chisel after removing the leg from the lathe. Alternatively, on a properly set up lathe, you can part off completely on the machine, letting the foot spin in your hand as you nudge the off button to shut off the lathe. The leg is now complete **(O)**.

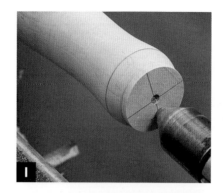

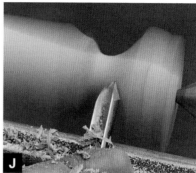

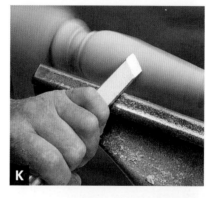

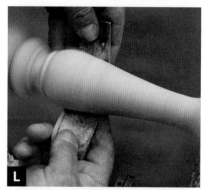

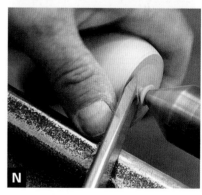

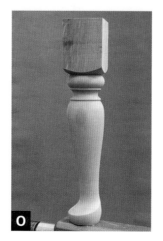

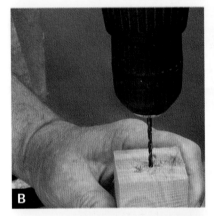

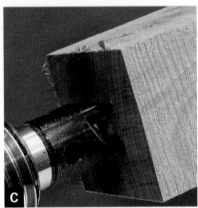

Split Turning

Sometimes you need identical halves of a spindle to use as a design element for furniture or architectural purposes. Sawing a spindle in half can be difficult and dangerous, and you won't get full half-rounds of identical cross-section. The traditional technique involves turning a blank assembled from two halves, which is split once the turning is completed. Paper is glued between the two halves to allow easy separation after turning.

Prepare the two halves for the blank, ensuring that the faces to be joined are flat. Spread glue on each face **(A)** and clamp the pieces together with a single sheet of thick, absorbent paper sandwiched in between. Allow the glue to dry thoroughly before turning.

Mount the blank with the join on the lathe axis. To prevent the centers from splitting the blank, drill a small shallow hole at center on each end **(B)**. In addition, align the four spurs of the drive on the diagonals of the square **(C)** and use a cup tail center **(D)**. For extra security with large split turnings, wrap square sections with tape or heavy rubber bands to prevent the blank disintegrating. As work progresses, move the tape or bands away from the areas to be cut.

When you've finished the spindle, part off at the tailstock end. Then split the turning from the drive end using a knife or chisel and mallet **(E, F)**. Sand away the paper on a disc sander, then reassemble the parts with rubber bands and twirl the end against a soft sanding disc mounted in a chuck **(G)**. You should end up with a pair of symmetrical halves **(H)**.

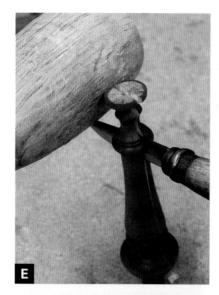

E

F

G

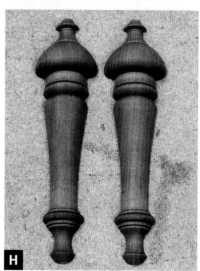

H

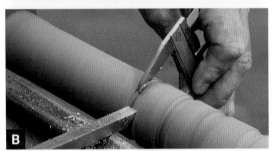

Cylinder

First use a roughing gouge to reduce the blank to near round, retaining remnants of the original square section **(A)**. Then use calipers and a parting tool or small scraper to set the required diameter every 2 in. (50mm) along the blank **(B)**. To reduce the risk of the caliper jaws scoring the blank, it pays to radius them slightly (see the photo on p. 48).

Now remove the waste between the calipered bands to create the cylinder. You might prefer to use a gouge, but generally you can do it all with a skew chisel, being sure to keep the skew bevel against the wood at all times. Take the first cut off one end **(C)** to establish a smooth surface against which the bevel can ride when starting the cut in the opposite direction. Then flip the tool over to make the long cut to the other end. For this, you can use the tool long point up with the handle near 90 degrees to the cylinder or long point down with the tool pointing in the direction you're cutting **(D)**. The skew chisel is easier to steer long point down, and there's less tool pressure against the blank.

Finally, eliminate any small bumps on the cylinder by sanding it with abrasive wrapped around a long sanding block **(E)**. Check your progress with a straightedge as you go.

Long Thin Spindles

Spiral chatter marks on a completed spindle indicate that it was flexing as you cut. There are two possible reasons for this. First, the tail center might be too tight; it should be adjusted to apply just enough pressure against the blank to support it without bending it. The second possibility is that you are pushing the tool too hard as you cut, deflecting the blank off its axis.

Any cutting pressure against a thin spindle needs to be equalized on the other side of the blank if it is to run true. You can use a mechanical steady, but a hand is much more convenient **(A, B)**.

On very slim spindles like lace bobbins or pens, you will need to support the blank throughout the turning **(C, D, E)**. While your upper (left) hand supports the wood, be sure it also maintains contact with both the rest and tool. If your fingers get too hot while using any of these grips, you'll know you're pushing the tool too hard into the cut. These grips, with the edge so close to the fingers, make novice turners extremely nervous, but I have never seen anyone cut from this situation. If the tool catches, it kicks back, not forward.

End-Grain Techniques, page 122

End-Grain Hollowing and Shaping, page 146

Chasing Threads, page 170

PART FOUR

Turning End Grain

A LOT OF INTERESTING SMALL PROJECTS involve working end grain. Many provide a good way of using up scraps of timber as you make boxes or knobs, or gifts for family and friends. You might even sell a few bits and pieces.

Blanks for what are essentially short center-work jobs—but in which the end grain is turned all the way to center—are best mounted in a chuck with no tail-center support. You'll see how to burrow into end grain using a gouge and scraper to create flowing curves and smooth surfaces straight off the tool. I also show ways of boring out deep thin-walled vessels.

You'll learn how to chase threads as well. This traditional skill allows for screwing parts together, which can save you heaps on stoppers for cruet sets, and will enhance your boxes, too. In fact, there are relatively few purely end-grain jobs, but the techniques are used whenever you need to part off a spindle cleanly or clean up the base of a goblet or hollow form.

End-Grain Techniques

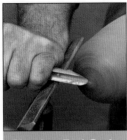

Shaping End Grain

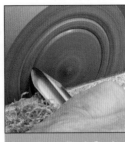

Detail on End Grain

End-Grain Projects

END-GRAIN BLANKS ARE short spindle blanks with the grain running the length of the blank and parallel to the lathe axis. And because the blanks are short and strength is rarely an issue, more interesting twisted or burly grain can be used.

This is center work, so all cuts across the grain are from the larger to smaller diameter. The domes and curves consist of half beads and half coves and are begun using standard center-work techniques, which are then modified to cut into center. Here, you'll see only the finishing cuts, as standard center-work techniques were explained in Section 10.

You can turn several pieces from a single blank, ensuring a consistent diameter on sets of knobs, for example, while speeding up production. The blank should not project from the chuck more than 8 in. (200mm), as any catch on the end tends to be catastrophic. Practice on blanks projecting no more than 4 in. (100mm) from the chuck.

End grain is difficult to cut cleanly. Problems arise mostly from cutting the wood faster than it wants to be cut. If you push the tool hard into the cut, you'll pluck fibers from the end grain, leaving a damaged surface. The secret to cutting end grain cleanly, as in all turning, is to let the wood come to the tool. The nearer you cut to the axis, the slower the wood is moving, so the rate at which you ease the tool forward should also be slower.

A typical end-grain blank is most easily and securely mounted in a long-jawed chuck.

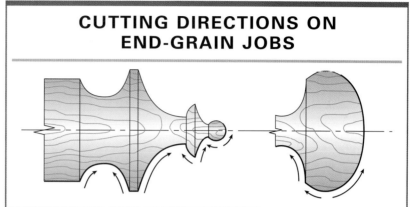

CUTTING DIRECTIONS ON END-GRAIN JOBS

Small, solid turnings can make good use of highly figured scraps regarded as waste by other woodworkers. I square up all off-cuts over 2 in. (50mm) thick into 3-in. (75mm) lengths or longer, then set them aside in cardboard boxes until thoroughly seasoned. If you are hoping to make your hobby pay for itself or if you are setting out as a full-time turner, you can make a good living turning small end-grain objects from scraps.

Longer blanks are ideal for small items, like spinning tops, in that several can be made from a single blank. Many end-grain jobs, like an egg, require rechucking for completion, whereas the knob project is turned on two fixings so you can undercut the back to fit flat against a door. (Knobs are mostly turned on one fixing.) The off-center exercise in this section introduces a technique you can use to create a limitless range of patterns and variations for use on inserts, medallions, or broaches.

A bilboquet, also known as a cup and ball, is a sort of fat goblet attached to a ball by a cord. It's an ancient game, in which the aim is to swing the ball into the air then catch it

As a full-time turner, you can make a good living turning small end-grain objects from blanks cut from offcuts.

on the cupped end. The ball is a sphere that is turned initially as center work, completed as face work, then sanded as something in between. A ball is about the only object for which a turner has to cut grain in every direction. Spheres can be a challenge if a matched set is needed; but a bilboquet ball doesn't demand that sort of accuracy.

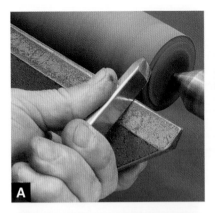

A

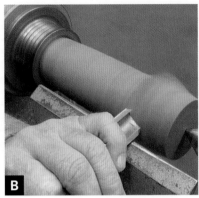

B

C

Skew chisel

Rest

D

E

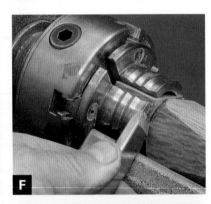

F

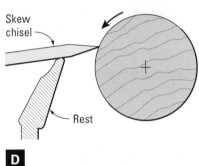

G

H

Roughing and Truing End Grain

Short lengths of end grain can be roughed down in a chuck using a roughing gouge, then smoothed to a cylinder using a skew chisel. If the blank protrudes from the chuck more than twice its diameter or if it includes cross-grain or burl, it's prudent to use tail-center support while roughing down.

For the most secure chucking of an end-grain blank, turn one end to a cylinder, then reverse the blank, mounting the cylindrical end in the chuck. Begin by fixing the square blank in the chuck, then start cutting at the far end with a gouge, working back toward the chuck in a series of scoops. After that, use a skew to smooth out the gouge marks.

▶ See *"Roughing to Round"* on p. 100.

Then true the end using a skew chisel **(A)**. Once the end is trued, reverse the blank in the chuck and again use the roughing gouge and skew to round the remaining square section (which had been in the chuck) **(B)**. A conventional shear cut may not produce a smooth surface on twisted grain or burl, as seen to the left in photo **C**. In such cases, try a peeling cut, as shown in photo **D**. Finally, remove the tail center and turn away the conical mark at the center **(E)**.

If the square blank seems secure in the chuck, there may be no point in reversing it. Instead, you can just part off the job, wasting the square section in the chuck. In that case, to prevent a frill of spiky fibers against the chuck, cut a V-groove close to the chuck **(F)** so the wood cuts away cleanly to the shoulder when roughing the cylinder **(G, H)**.

Flat End Grain

Flat surfaces can be turned using either a gouge or a skew chisel. Heavy cutting (to shorten a blank, for example) is best done with a fingernail gouge. Start the tool on its side with the bevel aligned in the direction of the cut **(A)**, then roll it slightly counterclockwise to use more of the edge, while keeping the left wing of the tool clear of the end grain **(B)**. Continue toward the center, slowing the pace of the cut and rolling the tool so it finishes on its side again at center **(C)**. You can also use this technique to create a slight hollow.

Turning end grain flat using a skew chisel is easier if the edge of the tool is slightly radiused. Begin by arcing the long point into the wood **(D)** (see drawing A on p. 101). As you move toward center, cut with the point of the chisel, keeping the edge clear of the work surface **(E)**. As you near center, raise the tool handle so you complete the cut using the portion of the edge just behind the point **(F)**. On most woods, you'll get a conical and often frilly shaving (seen here in miniature), which is unlike any other and fun to turn. The bevel will sometimes burnish dark lines on the end grain, but these will vanish with light sanding.

[TIP] A skew chisel used on flat end grain should be slightly radiused.

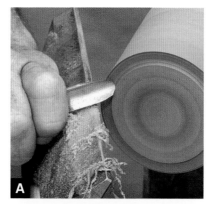
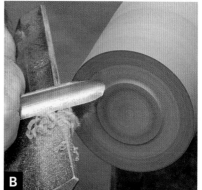

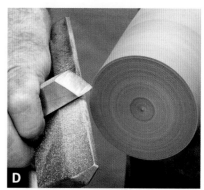
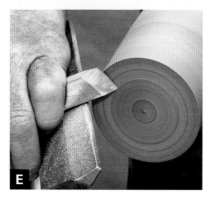

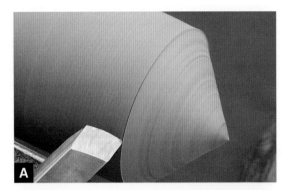

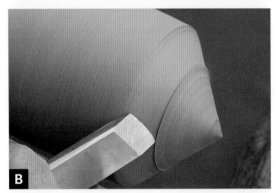

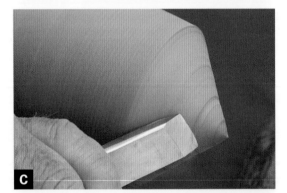

Cones

A cone can be cut using either a skew chisel or a gouge. Either tool follows the same path, as when turning flat end grain, but catches are less likely. A skew chisel requires less precision than a gouge when cutting the point of the cone.

Having roughed the cone to shape, start with the skew chisel's long point down, with the bevel aligned in the direction of the cut. Pivot the point through an arc into the wood; then about halfway across the surface **(A, B)**, gradually raise the handle so you begin cutting with the edge instead of the tip **(C)**. Ease the edge very gently across the axis to leave a sharp point. If you push the tool too fast into the wood, you'll pluck fibers from the end grain and fail to cut a sharp point. Burnish marks on the cut surface **(D)** will be removed with minimal sanding.

If using a detail gouge, start the gouge on its side and keep it that way as it arcs toward center. Slow the pace of the cut all the way to center, being sure to let the wood come to the tool to avoid tearing the grain. The cutting should be taking place mostly just below the nose of the tool (**E, F, G**). To slice off the very tip of the cone, use the curve at the center of the gouge tip (**H**).

To cut a concave cone, roll the gouge slightly counterclockwise for a heavier cut (**I**), continuing the roll as you cut to the point (**J, K**).

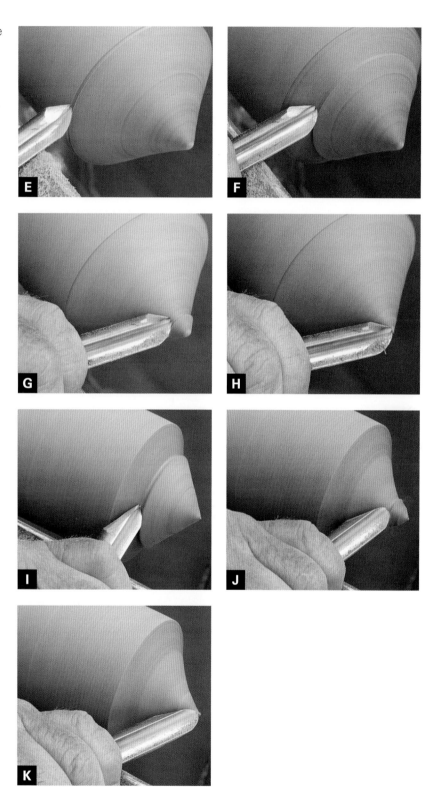

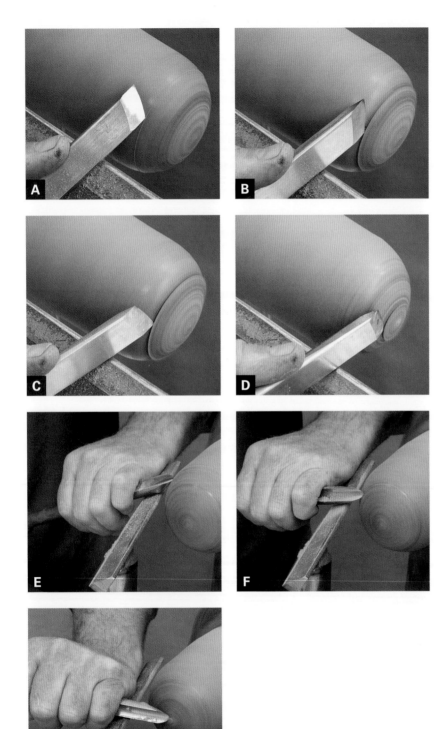

Domes

Domes can be cut using either a skew chisel or a detail gouge. Start the skew chisel long point up with the bevel rubbing **(A)**. Ease the tool along the rest using the short corner of the skew chisel as you roll into the curve **(B)**. Although you can continue to cut all the way to center in this position, it can be hard to see what you're doing. To remedy this, flip the skew over to use the long point **(C)**, raising the handle so you cut with the edge of the tool rather than the point **(D)**.

When using a gouge, position it with the flute up **(E)**, then roll it clockwise to start the cut **(F)**. Keep rolling until it ends up on its side at center **(G)**.

Ogee

To cut an ogee, use a detail gouge. Be sure to roll it so the portion of the edge that is cutting always remains at about 45 degrees to the oncoming wood.

Begin with the gouge on its side, with the bevel aligned in the direction of the cut **(A)**. Roll the flute slightly upward as you raise the handle to cut the concave section **(B)** and the shoulder **(C)**. Finally, roll the gouge back onto its side to complete the dome **(D)**.

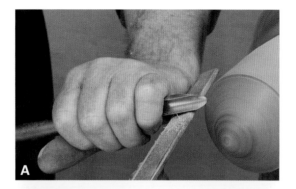

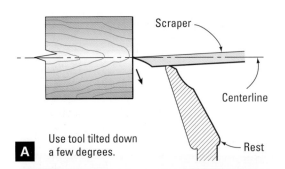

Scraper

Centerline

Rest

A Use tool tilted down a few degrees.

B

C

D

Scrapers on End Grain

A shear-cut surface can usually be improved by very gentle scraping. On flat or convex surfaces, use a skew chisel as a scraper. The edge of the chisel should have a slight radius. This allows you to use all of the edge at some time, while preventing the entire edge from contacting at once, which inevitably causes a catch. Raise the rest slightly so the scraper tilts downward when cutting at center height (**A**). That way, any catch will carry into space. Hold the tool flat on the rest and take very fine cuts, creating only tiny curly shavings and/or dust (**B**).

For scraping concave curves, I use an old skew chisel that can be reshaped as required and honed to leave a small burr on the upper side of the edge (**C**). The radius of the edge should be only slightly less than the curve you're scraping. Cut as gently as possible.

[**TIP**] **Scrape using a skewed edge whenever possible. Never have the tool at 90 degrees to the surface you're cutting if you can avoid it, and tilt the edge slightly below horizontal.**

To scrape into a corner at the bottom of a bead or shoulder, use the skew chisel's long point, being sure to keep the tool flat on the rest (**D**). Remember that you can flip the tool to get into the opposite corners.

Beads

Cut beads into end grain using a ⅜-in. (9mm) shallow-fluted detail gouge with a long fingernail grind. Begin with the gouge on its side, the flute facing away from the wood, and the bevel resting against the end grain. Swing the handle around so the nose of the tool pivots into the end grain **(A)**. Then take an arcing cut from the opposite direction **(B)**, pivoting the nose in from space without the bevel rubbing first. Make your cuts as light as possible, letting the wood come to the tool. Then, in the same manner, cut another groove going over the first one to begin to create a bead **(C, D)**. Finish up this inner groove by then coming in from the right **(E, F)**. Any facets left on the bead can be rounded over by light sanding **(G)**.

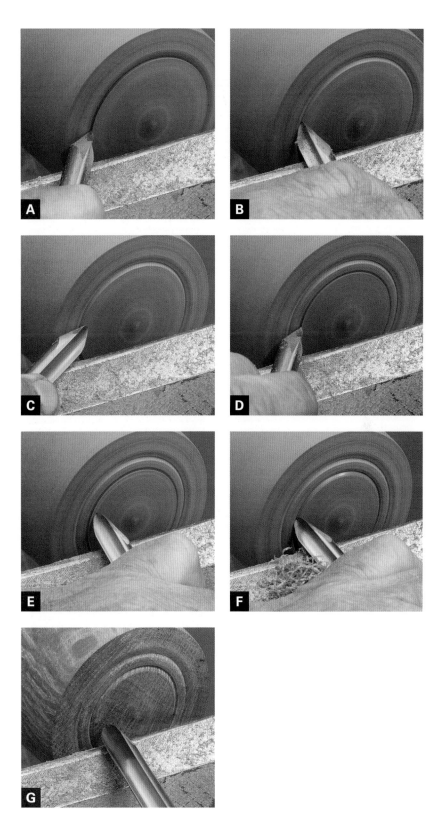

A

Standing Bead

To create a standing bead, first cut the bead, as shown in "Beads" on p. 131, then remove the surrounding material. Use a detail gouge to cut in from the rim **(A)**, then use a skew chisel flat on the rest to scrape away the waste in confined areas that the gouge cannot easily access **(B)**. Finally, scrape the surface on either side of the bead. If you go very gently **(C)**, you should end up with a silky-smooth surface **(D)**.

B

C

D

V-Grooves

To cut V-grooves on end grain, use the skew chisel as a scraper. Hold it on its side, flat on the rest, and tilt it down a degree or two, easing the point very gently into the wood **(A)**. You might need to back the rest slightly away from the end grain so the chisel sits on its side rather than on a portion of the bevel **(B)**.

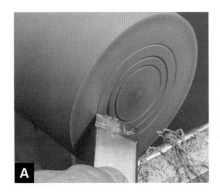
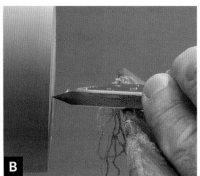

Small Finial

To turn small finials, you need a long-beveled detail gouge. Having roughed the bead/finial to size **(A)**, finish up the shape using the point of the gouge in a series of small downward-arcing cuts **(B, C)**, pivoting but not pushing the tool on the rest **(D)**.

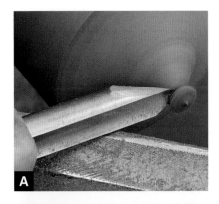
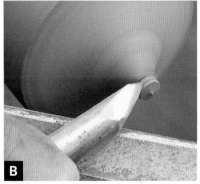
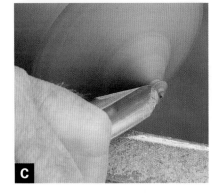
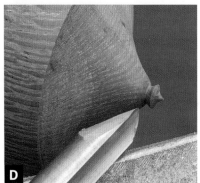

Set of Knobs

When making a set of knobs, it's important to ensure that they are consistent in diameter and length. Make each knob in a set the same way: Don't try a different technique halfway through, as that will affect the form. The 1⅛-in.- (28mm-) square blank for these knobs is securely gripped in the Vicmarc shark jaws. Therefore, only one fixing is required.

Turn the blank to a smooth cylinder. To avoid a fray of torn fibers against the chuck, cut a V-groove through to solid wood before cutting toward the chuck (see photos F–H on p. 124). Turn the end grain flat **(A)**. Set the diameter **(B, C)** and turn a cylinder. Then lay out the first knob, measuring from the flat end **(D)**.

This design has a beaded face, so lay out the bead **(E)** and turn the decoration using a ⅜-in.

(9mm) detail gouge **(F)**. Use a parting tool to set the depth of the knob and the diameter of the stem **(G)**, then complete the knob using the detail gouge **(H)**. Set the diameter of the tenon **(I)**, sand and finish the knob (but not the tenon) on the lathe, and part off using a narrow parting tool **(J)** or skew chisel's long point. To make the next knob, turn the end grain on the blank flat and repeat the process.

Spherical Knob

Mount the blank so the end that will be the back of the knob projects from the chuck. Use the skew chisel flat on the rest to peel away the shoulders **(A)**. When the blank is round, use a detail gouge to dish the end grain very slightly **(B)**; if the back of the knob is slightly undercut it will sit snugly against a door or other surface. Check with a straightedge or your gouge.

[TIP] **The back of a gouge can be used as a handy straightedge to quickly check the flatness of the end of a blank or other surface.**

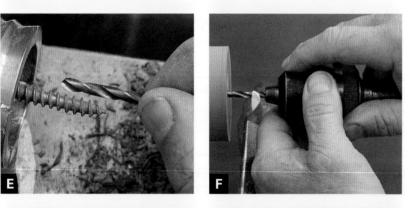

Refine the rim with a gentle scrape using the skew on its side **(C)**, then flip the skew and use the long point to turn a cone at the center for locating the drill **(D)**. Use a drill with a diameter equal to the screw shank **(E)** and drill the hole for the chuck screw **(F)**. You can mount the drill in the tailstock, but drilling freehand, with the drill in a Jacobs chuck or handle, is much faster. Use tape on the drill to gauge the desired depth.

Remount the blank on a screw chuck **(G)** and turn away the remaining square section **(H)**.

True the end flat **(I)**, then lay out the dimensions **(J)** and set the diameters **(K)**.

Next, turn the spherical portion **(L)**. You'll get a better finish on convex curves using a skew chisel rather than a gouge. But use a gouge to turn the half cove **(M)**, returning to the skew chisel for the groovy detail at the base **(N)**. Sand and polish on the lathe **(O)**.

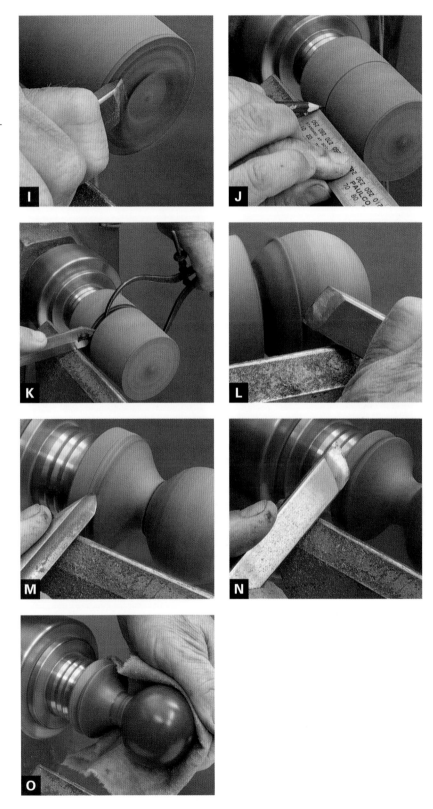

Egg

This is an ideal project for using up scraps of burl or, as here, cross-grained blanks not suitable for hollowing or thin sections. Eggs make a wonderful skew-chisel exercise. The key to a successful egg is turning smooth, parabolic curves with no bumps, dips, or pointy bits that could cause a laying bird pain.

Short blanks can be turned between centers, after which each end is completed with the egg mounted in a jam chuck. However, that approach involves three fixings. Instead, here I used a longer blank, allowing me to fix one end in a chuck while completely turning the other end. This way, there are only two fixings for the whole process. I began with a 2-in.- (50mm-) square blank, 8 in. (200mm) long, from which I got three eggs.

Shape the egg using a skew chisel (A), flipping to the long point across the end grain (B). Complete the exposed end before reducing the diameter at the other end to less than ½ in. (13mm), otherwise, you'll have chatter problems. If the grain picks out on the center section, take a delicate peel/scrape cut while keeping the skew flat on the rest (C).

Turn the other end with the skew's long point down (D), then sand all you can before polishing the half that will be mounted in a chuck (E). Part off using the long point of the skew (F). To avoid damage to the end grain, take care not to pull the egg away; catch the egg as the cut is completed.

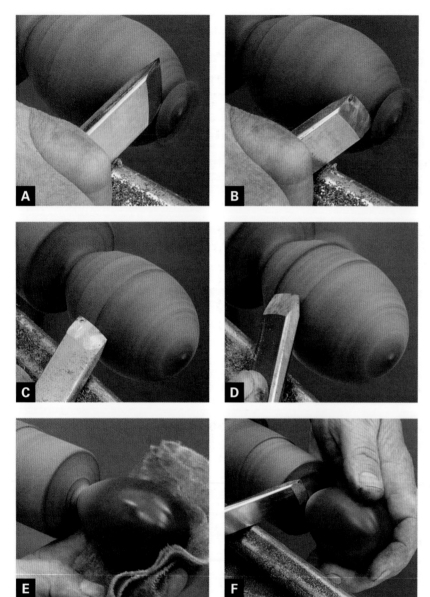

Make a jam chuck from a larger-diameter blank. Keep the wall thickness at least ¼ in. (6mm) and use soft wood, which will compress a bit around the egg. True the chuck blank **(G)** and measure the widest diameter of the egg **(H)**. Mark the diameter on the end grain **(I)**. Turn the hole very slightly smaller and keep the walls cylindrical for about ⅜ in. (9mm) into the opening **(J)**. Make the hole deep enough so the egg doesn't bottom out.

Push the egg firmly into the chuck, tapping it home if necessary with a small mallet or hammer. Then complete the turning using the skew's long point **(K)**. Finally, sand and polish the end **(L)**, then remove the egg by tapping the chuck with a large wrench or other heavy object **(M)**.

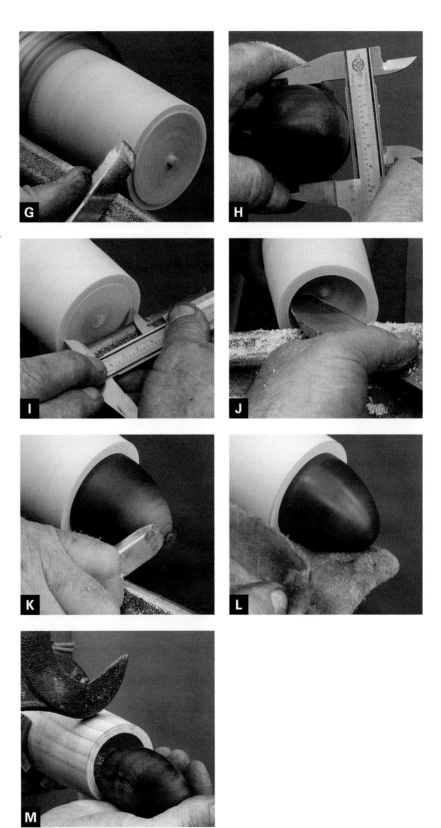

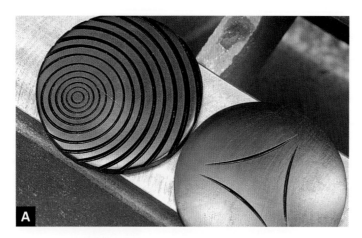

A

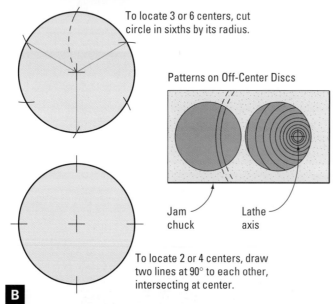

To locate 3 or 6 centers, cut circle in sixths by its radius.

Patterns on Off-Center Discs

Jam chuck

Lathe axis

To locate 2 or 4 centers, draw two lines at 90° to each other, intersecting at center.

B

C

Off-Center Decorations

Geometrical patterns can be created using an offset chuck. The technique is ideal for decorating box lids, rosettes, or inserts. Mounting a disc in an off-set chuck causes the disc to swing in an orbit around the lathe axis. A tight orbit allows cutting concentric circles, some of which intersect the rim **(A)**. With a wider orbit, all cuts intersect the rim **(B)**. By rotating the position of the disc within the chuck, you can create designs that incorporate various centers, such as a triple-arc design **(A)**, which involves three centers. I'll use this second design to demonstrate the process.

To make the disc, first turn a cylinder with a slight dome on the end, then part off a 3/16-in.- (5mm-) thick disc. Using a template, lay out the three arcs, carrying the center for each one over to the opposite edge of the disc **(C)**. Alternatively, you can lay out any number of centers that you like. To locate three or six centers, divide a circle in six by its radius, join the intersections at center, and project them onto the disc edge **(B)**. To lay out four centers, create two lines at 90 degrees to each other, intersecting at the center of the disc. You might also find it useful to mark the center of the disc with pencil, to use as an aid when relocating the chuck and disc later.

Next, cut a squared rectangular block for the chuck. The length of the chuck will depend on the patterns you want, but it should not be longer than three times its width. Scrap medium-density fiberboard (MDF) at least 3/4 in. (19mm) thick is ideal for disposable one-off chucks, because it's flat and of consistent thickness. Before turning the rebate, saw a groove about 3/8 in. (9mm) deep up the center so you can insert a lever beneath the chucked disc to remove it. Set calipers to the disc's diameter **(D)** and transfer that measurement to one end of the off-set chuck **(E)**. Then turn a straight-sided recess with a depth slightly less than the thickness of the disc **(F)**. When done, the disc must fit tightly in the recess. (This is a recycled chuck: During a previous project, I had to turn the surface down somewhat to leave a disc proud, hence the slope around the recess.)

When the recess is finished, move the chuck off center. You can hold and relocate the jam chuck on a screw chuck, but the slightest catch can ease it off center. You can also use a faceplate, but a better approach is to remove two jaws on a self-centering chuck and mount the jam chuck block between them. It will be off-balance, so start with slow speeds—half or less than those recommended in the chart on p. 99.

Press the disc firmly into the recess with a center-line aligned with one edge of the groove **(G)**. Mark that edge with a cross, as the other layout lines must be set to the same point when the disc is rotated to make the remaining arcs. Before cutting into the disc, do a test run in pencil to ensure the cut will lie where you want it. You might also find it helpful to mark the cutting line on the rest for an accurate entry cut.

[**TIP**] **To create off-set circles, move the center less than half the radius of the disc. For incised lines that intersect the rim of the disc, move the center more than half the radius.**

Cut the first arc using a spear-point scraper. You can barely see what you are cutting at first, so proceed very cautiously. Ensure that the scraper is tilted down. Better still, pivot the point upward into the cut from below. It's helpful if the chuck and disc are two different colors so you can tell

D

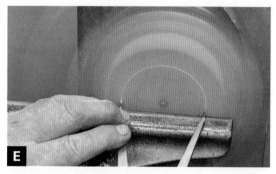

E

F

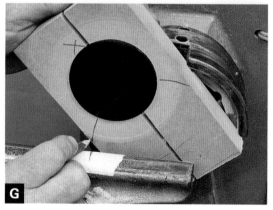

G

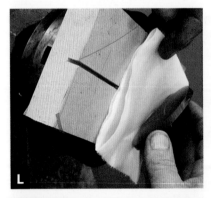

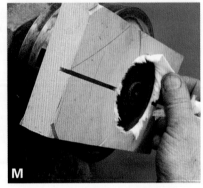

what you're cutting by the color of the dust being thrown. Stop the lathe occasionally to check progress **(H)**.

Reposition the disc in the chuck for the second and third cuts, aligning each of the remaining centerlines with the edge of the groove as before **(I)**. The groove also enables you to pry the disc free by inserting an old dental tool or other prying device beneath the disc **(J)**.

For a final sanding and polishing, return the chuck to center **(K)**. Concentric decoration can also be added now if desired.

You can turn the other side by reversing the disc in the jam chuck. Here the fit was a shade sloppy, requiring a double layer of two-ply toilet paper to get a tight fit **(L)**. Tear away the surplus **(M)** before turning the back **(N)**. The center boss was left for mounting a broach pin.

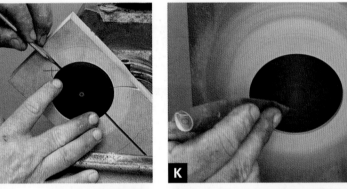

Bilboquet

The ball for this bilboquet includes a hole in which to store the spindle. Or you might say that the spindle has a spike on which to store the ball **(A)**. For the ball, you'll need a blank that is slightly longer than the ball's diameter. You'll also need two larger, similarly proportioned blocks of waste wood for chucks. This ball of about 3 in. (75mm) in diameter works well and it's not too difficult to make.

Begin by mounting the ball blank in a four-jaw chuck or cup chuck, and true it to an accurate cylinder with flat end grain. Then mark a length from the end equal to the diameter **(B)**. First divide this in half, then mark the center of each half. The marks need to be accurate, so lay them out with the lathe off **(C)**, then hold a pencil to each mark and spin the wood by hand **(D)**. Mark a circle on the end grain halfway between the center and the rim. Then cut a straight chamfer between the two lines **(E)**. On the opposite end, part in and mirror the layout and cuts **(F)**. To locate the circle halfway between the center and the rim, take the distance between the two lines remaining on the cylinder and measure in from the rim. After chamfering both ends, part off the roughed sphere.

Next, you'll need to make a chuck to hold the sphere for rounding. To ascertain how large a blank you need for the chuck, first use calipers to determine the maximum diameter of the ball (corner to corner, not facet to facet) **(G)**. Then add ¾ in. (19mm) or so, so the chuck wall will be about ⅜ in. (9mm) thick. A softish wood like poplar is ideal.

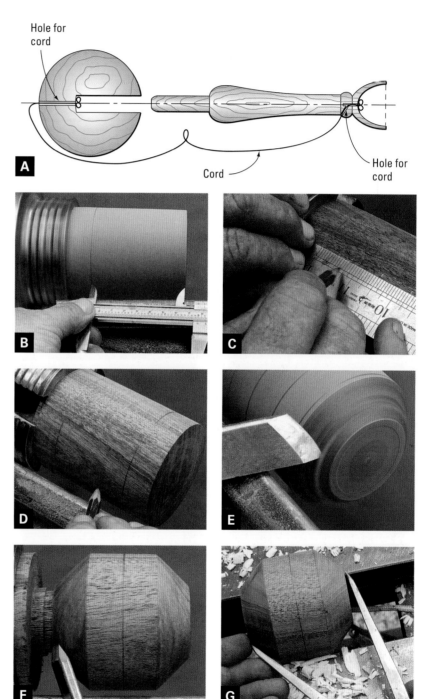

Hole for cord

Cord

Hole for cord

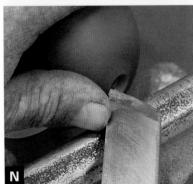

After you've trued the chuck blank to a cylinder with a flat end, transfer the maximum diameter of the roughed sphere to the end of the chuck blank (H), then hollow using a gouge and scrapers. The hollow needs to be tapered inward about 1 degree. Push the sphere into the chuck by hand, centering the original centerline in the chuck. To check this, put a pencil on the end grain near the center, and spin the job by hand. This should result in a circle split in half by the center-line (I). After it's aligned, tap the sphere firmly into the chuck using a small hammer, then recheck the alignment.

The sphere's grain is now oriented as face work, so remove the waste by working from center outward. Proceed cautiously until the centerline remains on a narrow flat band (J). Then refine the surface by shear scraping, using a spear-point scraper to work just inside the rim of the chuck (K). Continue until the pencil line is barely discernible. You will have now created one hemisphere. Remove the workpiece by tapping the chuck with something heavy like a lathe wrench, a heavy scraper, or a small hammer.

Now make a smaller jam chuck to grip the hemisphere just turned. Tap the finished hemisphere into the chuck, again with the original centerline centered on the axis (L). You can also use the tail center to check alignment. Turn down to the original centerline to complete the sphere (M). When you're done, sand very lightly, rechucking the sphere frequently, always rotating it to a different position. For sanding, the ball doesn't need to be quite so firmly in the chuck because your hand (holding the abrasive) will be there to prevent it from flying out.

Finally, align the ball in the chuck with the grain parallel to the axis, so you can drill the holes for the cord and spindle. First make a starter cone (N), then drill the small hole all the way through for the cord (O). Then use a ½-in. (13mm) drill mounted in a Jacobs chuck in the tailstock to enlarge this hole two-thirds of the way through the ball **(P)**.

The spindle part to the bilboquet is a sort of fat goblet with a spiky base. This cup is 2 in. (50mm) in diameter, with the entire length of the spindle being 7½ in. (190mm) long.

Once you have trued the spindle blank, begin by hollowing the end **(Q)**. For the cord, drill a small-diameter hole about ½ in. (13mm) deep **(R)** that will connect with another hole coming up and in from the side. Sand the inside of the bowl.

Complete the bowl **(S)** before slimming down the spindle. Then finish turning the handle **(T)**. Drill a small hole up into center to connect with the hole in the cup **(U)**. Finally, turn the spike to fit into the hole in the ball **(V)**, then sand and finish on the lathe **(W)**.

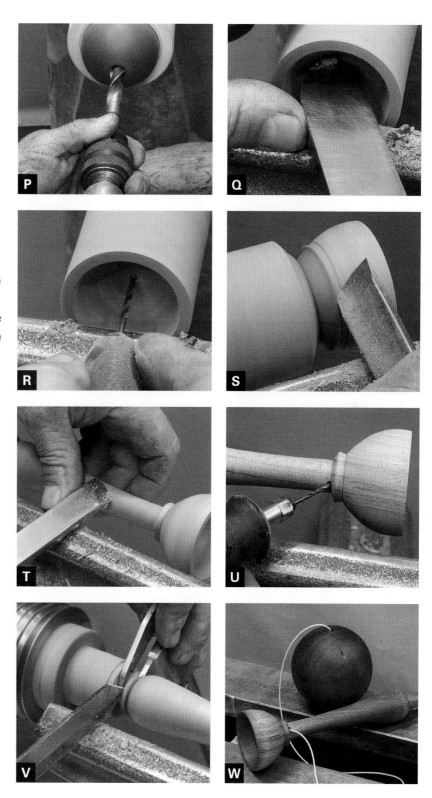

End-Grain Hollowing and Shaping

Rough Hollowing

➤ Preliminary Drilling (p. 149)

➤ Hollowing with a Gouge (p. 150)

➤ Boring with Scrapers (p. 151)

Internal Shaping

➤ Cylinders (p. 152)

➤ Rounded Hollows (p. 153)

➤ Undercut Rims (p. 154)

➤ Deep Boring (p. 155)

End-Grain Projects

➤ Vase (p. 156)

➤ Hollow Form (p. 159)

➤ Lamp Base (p. 162)

➤ Goblet (p. 164)

➤ Box (p. 167)

THE TECHNIQUE YOU USE to hollow into end grain will depend on the depth to which you are hollowing, the form you're turning, and the diameter of the opening through which you are working. When hollowing end grain, you're usually cutting well away from the rest, so keeping control of the leverage will be your main problem. The farther you cut from the rest, the greater the likelihood of a catch. Therefore, tools need to be substantial to eliminate vibration, with ever longer handles to counteract catches as you go deeper. Keep your weight over the tool with the

handle aligned beneath your forearm. You need to be prepared for some big catches and destroyed work when you begin to hollow end grain. Wear an impact-resistant face shield.

When rough hollowing, you can take one of two approaches. The first is to drill a depth hole, then shear cut outward from the hole. The second approach is to push the tools straight into end grain. Shearing cuts are more difficult to learn, but they generally remove waste a lot faster and leave a cleaner surface than pushing tools straight into end grain.

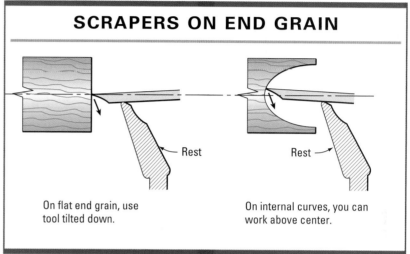

SCRAPERS ON END GRAIN

On flat end grain, use tool tilted down.

On internal curves, you can work above center.

Rest

Rest

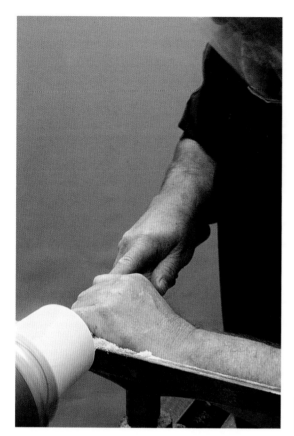

When deep hollowing, keep your weight over the tool with the handle aligned beneath your forearm.

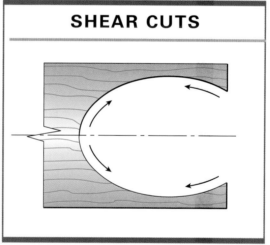

SHEAR CUTS

End-grain hollowing requires sharp edges because it is particularly unforgiving of blunt tools and aggressive cutting. Catches can pluck chunks from the end grain to a depth of $\frac{1}{16}$ in. (1.5mm). Such damage is impossible to skim smooth in a single cleanup pass. Lengths of side grain also tear easily, so final cuts need to be ever more delicate until finally the edge merely strokes the surface.

Tools cutting flat end grain or on center must be tilted down a few degrees to avoid catches. On curves, they can cut well above center and be tilted at an angle so the edge begins to shear the fibers, leaving a smoother surface. To shear cut the fibers on internal curves, the cut moves away from the lathe axis, as shown in the drawing just above.

The three generic end-grain projects that seem to be of most fascination are goblets, lidded containers (often called *boxes*), and vases. Goblets continue a centuries-long tradition that began before the Industrial Revolution, when turned wooden beakers and other forms of drinking vessel were common. Boxes, too, have long been turned to contain all manner of spices, snuff, needles, tobacco, and pills—indeed, anything small or loose that needs a container. And a

Hollowed forms can
make fine vases for
dried-flower
arrangements. Tall,
thin vases are best
kept heavy so they
don't topple.

box base without a lid makes an ideal pot for storing pencils and pens.

Vases, however, are a modern phenomenon, particularly the deep hollow forms that mimic glass and ceramic forms. These are not easy to make. With their thin walls and narrow openings, they have a considerable "Wow! How-did-they-do-that?" factor. But I suspect no old-time turner would have wasted much time or hard-won material on so frivolous an object more easily made from clay, glass, or even metal. Lamp bases are a more traditional variation on the vase theme, derived as they so often are on ceramic forms. The examples in this section could be used as vases if the drilled hole stopped short of the base.

Preliminary Drilling

You can drill a depth hole by hand using a depth drill (see photos A–C on p. 53). However, wider depth holes can be made with a drill fixed in the tail center with the lathe running no faster than 1000 rpm, and slower if the diameter demands (see chart on p. 99). Here, a 1¾-in.- (45mm-) diameter sawtooth bit mounted in a Jacobs chuck is used to remove the core of a vase **(A)**. As the drill vanishes into the hole, shavings jam up around the drill shank, so you need to back the drill out, turn the lathe off, and crumble the debris clear **(B)**.

To go deeper than the length of the drill, first mark the tail-shaft spindle to gauge the depth of the hole **(C)**. Wind the tail center back; then, with the lathe switched off, push the drill into the hole as far as it will go **(D)**. Lock the tail center to the lathe bed, start the lathe, and wind in the drill **(E)**. You'll need to clear the jammed shavings frequently by sliding the tailstock back. This can be done with the lathe running if you keep at least half the drill head in the hole.

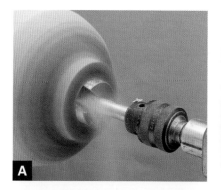

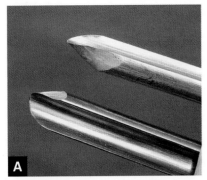

A

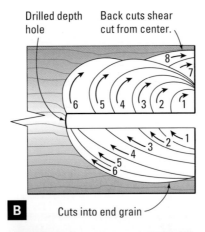

Drilled depth hole

Back cuts shear cut from center.

B

Cuts into end grain

C

D

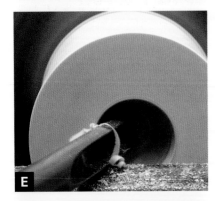

E

F

G

Hollowing with a Gouge

By far the quickest technique for removing waste to a depth of about 3 in. (75mm) is back hollowing with a shallow gouge (rather than a shallower-fluted detail gouge). The shape of the edge and length of the bevel are crucial; you need a long bevel and a convex fingernail edge devoid of straight sections **(A)**.

After drilling a depth hole, make a series of initial hollowing cuts—cuts 1 to 6 in the upper half of drawing **B**. To make cut 1, begin with the gouge on its side at the center, and nose it into the depth hole **(C)**. Pull the handle back and down as you roll the tool slightly clockwise, so it cuts almost upside down and away from the center at about two o'clock **(D)**. Then return to the center and make subsequent cuts in the same manner, keeping the opening much smaller than the interior **(E, F)**. When you've reached the required depth, open up the rim with cuts 7 and 8.

An alternative approach is to cut into the end grain from the rim, hollowing as shown in the lower half of **B**. In this case, rest the gouge on its side with the flute toward center, rotating the gouge slightly counterclockwise to take a larger shaving as you head for the depth hole **(G)**.

Boring with Scrapers

You can hollow directly against the end grain using scrapers as boring tools, but using no more than ½ in. (13mm) of an edge at one time **(A)**. Set the rest so that when the tool is horizontal, the top is above center with the lower left side clear of the wood, as shown in drawing **B**. Ease the tool forward so you get a thin ribbon shaving **(C)**. Never use all of the edge at once, even on a narrow tool, and reduce the width of cut the farther you are from center.

Using a round-nose scraper, first push into the center, then ease the edge away from the center and pull back toward the rim in a series of sweeping passes **(D)**. Use no more than ½ in. (13mm) of the edge at one time **(E)**. If you use the whole edge at once, it will catch.

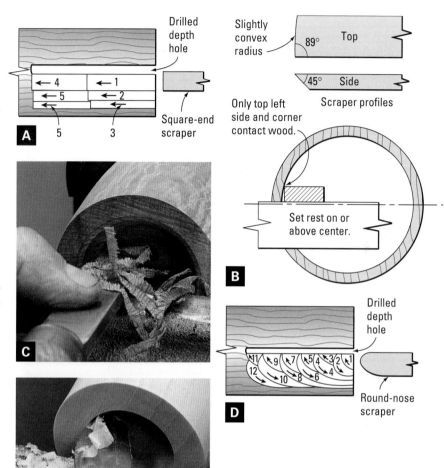

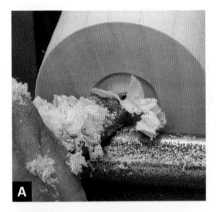

A

B

C

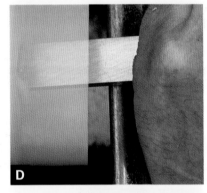

D

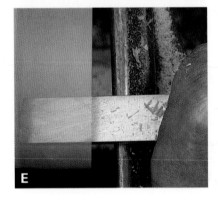

E

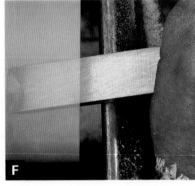

F

Cylinders

Small cylindrical holes are best drilled using a sawtooth drill mounted in the tailstock, as shown in the photos on p. 149. However, the tail center must be accurately aligned on the lathe axis. Drill center-spurs mark the end grain, but these can be turned away, or hidden by leather or flocked discs. You can also bore right through to create a tube, then block the end with a turned insert.

You can hollow a cylinder using a square-end scraper with a barely acute left corner (about 89 degrees) and a slightly radiused edge (see **B** on p. 151). Set the rest high enough that only the left corner contacts the side of the hollow. Angle the tool, using the left corner for the initial cut into the center **(A)**, then bring the blade parallel to the axis **(B)**. Boring with the edge partially across center, you can push the tool quite hard because the pressure is absorbed by the chuck. At the center, the cutting edge of the tool is pitched down no more than 3 degrees below horizontal, and the hole you cut narrows inward from the opening. To turn a cylindrical hole, you need to keep the tool blade horizontal and parallel to the lathe axis **(C)**.

To turn the end grain flat and smooth, use the left corner of the scraper to cut a series of steps moving left from center **(D)** into the corner **(E)**. Then swing the edge right and take a very light cut back to center using the middle of the slightly radiused edge **(F)**. (Note: For clarity, half of the blank was cut away to create the x-ray effect.)

Rounded Hollows

Finishing cuts in a rounded hollow are made by cutting inward from the rim **(A)**, then outward from the bottom back to the rim **(B)** (see "Shear Cuts" on p. 147). To reduce vibration when cutting at the rim, keep your thumb against the side of the tool blade as a fulcrum, and your fingers on the wood behind the tool edge. Start the scraper tilted up, so it is shear scraping at the rim **(C)**. Then raise the handle to bring the tool horizontal as you cut into the curve **(D)**. Complete the curve from the bottom, starting with the gouge pitched down at center **(E)**, then lean on the handle and push it away from you to bring the tool back to horizontal (and above center) to cut a smooth curve **(F)**.

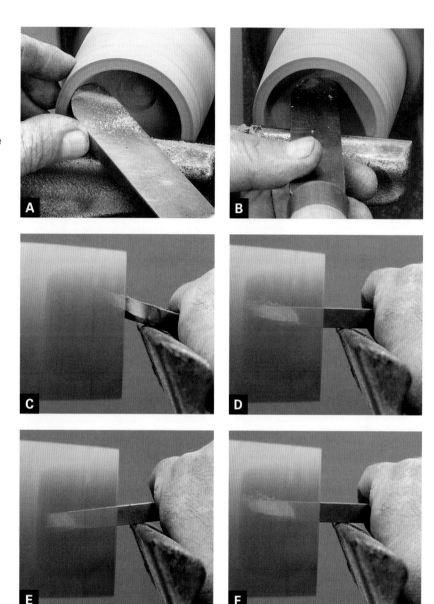

A

B

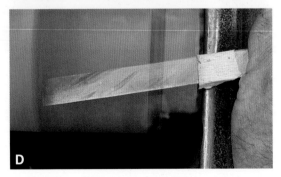

C

D

Undercut Rims

Designs for small boxes and vases frequently incorporate an interior that's wider than the opening, resulting in an interior shoulder. To cut under the shoulder, you need a side scraper. Although these are commercially available in various shapes, you can easily grind the exact shape you need from an old planer blade or scraper.

First drill the center to the overall depth of the hollow and turn as much as you can with a square-end scraper **(A)**. On a small scale, a homemade scraper—like this one ground from an elderly 1-in. (25mm) scraper—can cut the shoulder and then the side **(B)**. Keep the full width of the tool on the rest. If you have the narrow neck on the tool rest, the edge tends to catch. Note that the long side edge is curved and that only a small portion is used at one time. Flat end grain and a square corner can be turned using the same scraper **(C)** or a slightly skewed square-end scraper **(D)**. The marked tape on the tool indicates depths.

Deep Boring

Larger-scale undercutting is done with heavy boring bars or bent scrapers with long, heavy handles **(A)**. Some hollowing systems, like this Dave Reeks hollow form system, include rests designed to prevent catches **(B)**.

When using bent scrapers, set the tool rest back from the job so the straight shaft of the tool sits on the rest **(C, D)**.

Boring bars have off-set cutters that are un-supported when the force of the wood bears on them. When using a boring bar freehand, start with the cutter pitched down about 30 degrees, then roll the edge up into the cut gradually so you can get used to the pressure of the wood **(E)**.

A boring system with a slotted tool rest as in **B** will prevent an off-set edge from catching. Set the slotted rest so that when the tool is horizontal the cutting edge is just above center, then adjust the front tool rest so the edge cuts at center. You'll need to readjust the front rest as you work farther into the hollow.

Cutters on the bar can be changed or adjusted as required. Here, a round-nose cutter was best for scraping the shoulder **(F)**. A narrower cutter proved much faster for hogging out the bulk of the waste on the side **(G)**. However, it needed to be swiveled to cut effectively into the end grain toward the base **(H)**.

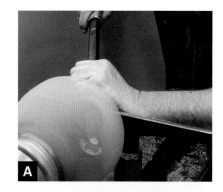

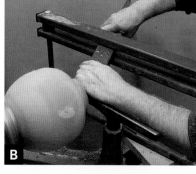

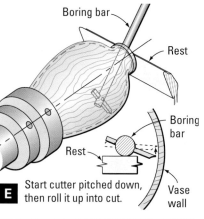

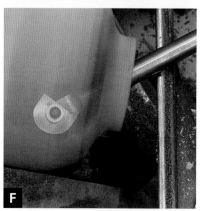

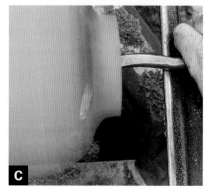

Start cutter pitched down, then roll it up into cut.

Boring bar

Rest

Boring bar

Rest

Vase wall

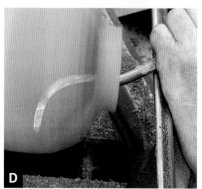

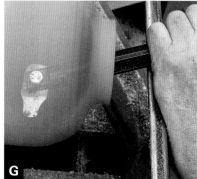

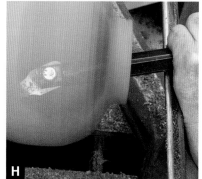

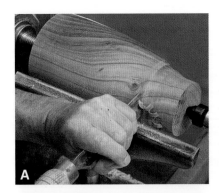

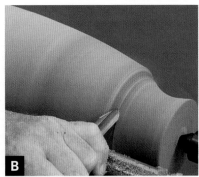

Vase

Begin with the blank between centers **(A)** and shape the form to include a base or short tenon you can fit into a chuck. This blank is turned to fit 5-in.- (125mm-) diameter jaws; but if you turn a tenon for rechucking, make it as a wide as your chuck jaws can expand, so you get the best grip. Smooth the body of the vase using a skew chisel and rough out the neck with a shallow gouge **(B)**.

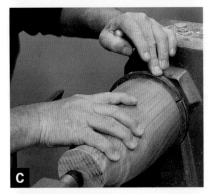

Remount the job in a chuck using the tail center to ensure accurate mounting **(C)**, then begin hollowing by drilling a wide depth hole, retaining about ⅝ in. (16mm) thickness at the base **(D)**. Leave the neck thick as you bore out the body **(E)**. Shavings, which clog the space every few seconds, are most easily removed with a blast of compressed air. Shaking or levering them out with a stick is tedious. (An advantage of turning art pieces with holes in the side is that the shavings are easier to remove.)

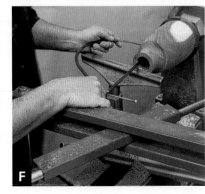

Measure the wall thickness frequently to gauge your progress **(F)**. As the wall gets thinner the sound of the cut rises in pitch, but you'll need to ruin a few pieces to learn exactly what a cutting sound can mean. With art pieces that include holes, you can actually see much of the wall thickness.

When the body is turned down to size, refine the inside of the neck using a round-nose scraper **(G)**, then sand as far inside the neck as you can reach **(H)**. Only after the inside has been completed should you finish detailing the neck profile. Use a detail gouge for this **(I)**, testing the thickness as you go. Then sand the upper part of the vase.

Now you'll need to remount the job between centers and turn away the chuck marks or the tenon on the foot. To do this, you'll need to make a jam chuck. Measure the internal diameter of the neck **(J)** and turn a tapered tenon to fit inside it **(K, L)**. Then mount the job between centers **(M)**.

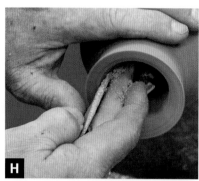

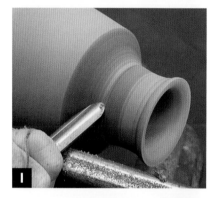

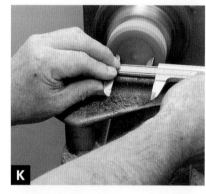

If the grain is anything less than straight, a gentle peeling cut **(N)** is much safer than a shear cut. If the remnants of jaw marks are difficult to remove, hide them in a V-groove cut with the skew chisel's long point **(O)**.

Use a detail gouge to turn the base slightly concave so the vase sits on its rim **(P)**. Use a skew chisel on its side to add decorative grooves **(Q)**. Sand, then wax and polish everywhere, except at the center of the base where the nub still needs to be removed. Last, sand away the nub **(R)** to complete the job **(S)**.

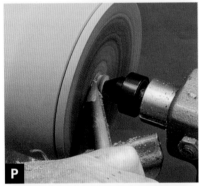

Hollow Form

Hollowing out a form through a very small hole at the top is difficult. However, there is an alternative approach—a trick in which you actually do your hollowing through a larger opening made in the bottom, then insert a plug to disguise it. The plug sits in a recess in the opening **(A)**.

To ensure the illusion, it's important that the grain on the plug lines up as well as possible with the grain on the perimeter of the opening. Therefore, begin by selecting a blank that has straight grain on one end. This will be the bottom of the form and the end from which you take the plug. The matching straight grain will help conceal the join later.

Begin the turning by roughly shaping the vase between centers, leaving a fat tenon at the top to fit your chuck **(A)**. Then mount this tenon in a chuck and use tail-center support while you turn the shoulders on the base. The central shoulder, which will be the plug, must be straight sided and smaller in diameter than the base before you part it free **(B)**.

After parting the plug free, measure its diameter **(C)**, and transfer that measurement to the end grain **(D)**. Drill the depth hole using a wide drill mounted in the tailstock **(E)**. Hollow within the diameter of the plug; then proceed with scrapers **(F)**, measuring as you go **(G)**. Take great care not to make the opening larger than the plug or the retaining shoulder.

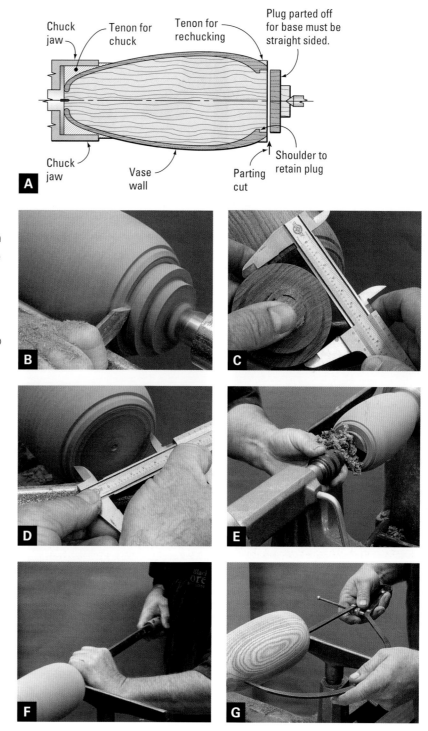

A — Chuck jaw · Tenon for chuck · Tenon for rechucking · Plug parted off for base must be straight sided. · Chuck jaw · Vase wall · Parting cut · Shoulder to retain plug

Next turn the recess for the plug **(H)**. Keep a small amount of end grain as a retaining shoulder **(A)** to prevent pushing the plug through the hole. When the plug fits, align the grain and draw a reference line across the join **(I)**.

While you can still measure the wall thickness, refine the profile, being sure to retain the rechucking tenon at the bottom **(J)**. Then glue the plug in place using cyanoacrylate adhesive, because of its quick curing properties. The pencil line provides your reference. Use a detail gouge to turn the base slightly concave **(K)** while retaining the center nub. To help conceal the join, hide it in a V-groove. Then cut in another groove or two to confuse the eye **(L)**.

Reverse the vase in the chuck, and complete the upper profile **(M)**. Turn a cone in the top using a small detail gouge **(N)**, then use a depth drill to

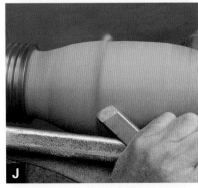

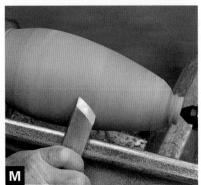

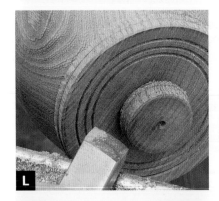

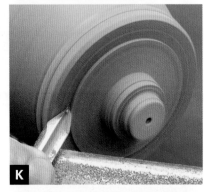

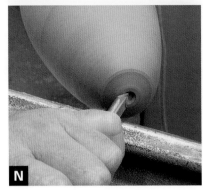

break through to the hollow **(O)**. Refine the opening using a small round-nose scraper **(P)**. At this point, sand, wax, and polish as much of the form as you can.

Finally mount the form between centers, with the opening toward the headstock. You can use a steel cone (as here), but a turned wood cone grips better. Also, a wood cone can be turned to fit any size opening, even those larger than your metal center. (To turn a cone, follow the same basic procedures you use to turn a jam chuck; see p. 79 and photos K–M on p. 157.) Beware of overtightening the tailstock, as the thin end grain in the base cannot take much pressure. Once mounted, remove the remaining fixing shoulder **(Q)**.

Complete the sanding and finishing, then remove the nub on the bottom. If you're feeling confident, you can part it off **(R)**. Otherwise use a sander to complete the job **(S, T)**.

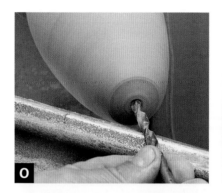

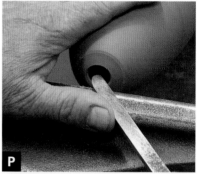

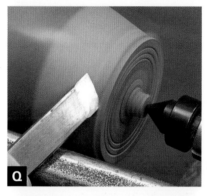

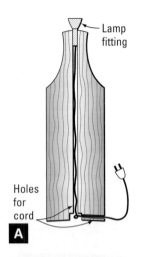

Lamp fitting

Holes for cord

A

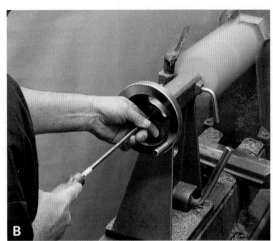

B

C

D

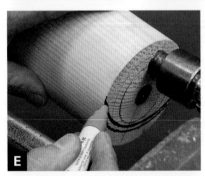

E

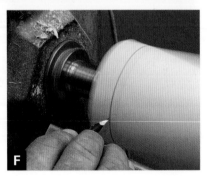

F

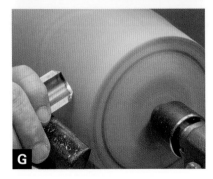

G

Lamp Base

A lamp base is a fat spindle with a hole drilled through the axis for a power cord that enters from the side. The holes meet in a wide recess in the base **(A)**. This 4-in.- (100mm-) diameter lamp is a 13-in- (330mm-) tall tapered oval turned on three centers.

Mount the blank so the bottom of the lamp is against the drive center. Drill a ⅜-in. (9mm) cord hole through the axis on the lathe using an auger through a hollow tail-center. Drill as near as you can to the spur drive without actually meeting it, withdrawing the auger frequently to clear the waste **(B)**.

[**TIP**] **Holes bored on the lathe are rarely dead accurate, as the wood grain pushes the auger off center.**

Take the blank off the lathe and use a spade bit to drill a rebate at the center about 1 in. (25mm) deep into the base to meet the center hole **(C)**. Ideally the rebate will be the same size as your spur drive, but if the auger traveled a long way off center, you'll need to drill a wider hole. (You'd also need to retain a hint of the first hole to center the spur drive.) Using a ⅜-in. (9mm) bit, drill the second cord hole in from the side of the blank, making sure that the hole intersects the rebate.

Remount the blank between centers, with the spur drive in the bottom rebate and a conical tail center at the other end. Turn the blank to a cylinder, then use a gouge to cut the base slightly concave so it will sit on its rim **(D)**. Go to the tailstock end and, with the piece spinning, touch the end grain with a pencil about midway between center and the perimeter. Then remove the blank from the lathe and draw a line through center so it cuts the circle twice. The two points at which the line intersects the circle will be the centers for the subsequent off-axis mountings.

Using a cup center to prevent the wood from splitting, relocate the center to one of the off-axis intersections. Rotate the workpiece by hand and mark an arc about ¼ in. (6mm) outside the circle **(E)**. Don't draw the arc inside the circle or you'll remove the intersection point for turning the next axis. Because you'll cut to this line, it needs to be dark and well defined. Near the opposite end of the blank, draw a reference line in soft pencil where the wood runs true, which will be in the "valley" between the two blurred areas and in line with the bottom of the rebate in the base **(F)**.

Now you're ready to create the tapered oval shape. Using a roughing gouge, make a straight cut connecting the arc line at the tail-center end with the reference line at the drive-center end **(G)**. Then use a heavy skew to smooth the surface, shear cutting from left to right **(H)**. Relocate the lamp top (at the tailstock end) to the opposite intersection and mark the new arc to be cut **(I)**. Also re-mark the true-running surface near the base, now in the center of the blurry area. Then turn the second taper as you did the first.

After turning the tapers, return the blank to its center mounting and turn the neck using a heavy gouge **(J)**. Clean up the top with the skew long point **(K)**, tightening the tailstock to take up any slack after the cut. Then sand the neck **(L)**.

Finish up by sanding the sides. If you use an orbital sander **(M)**, the two sides will be sharply defined, as at the right in **N**. If you want rounded edges, sand with the lathe running slowly at about 300 rpm.

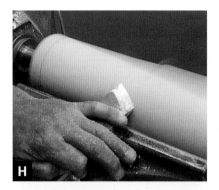

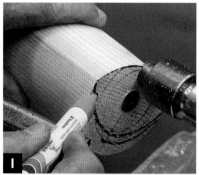

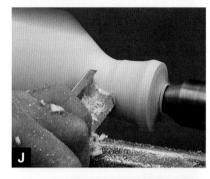

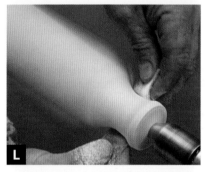

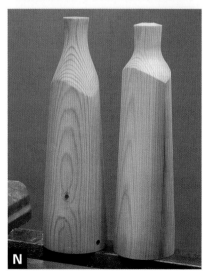

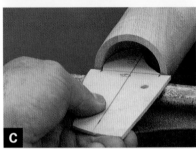

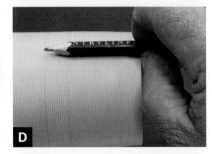

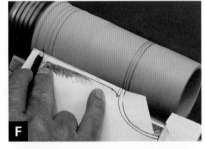

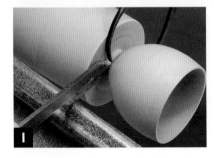

Goblet

With any goblet or variation on the form, complete the inside of the bowl before starting on the outside. Then complete the outside of the bowl before shaping the stem. This way, you retain the bulk of the blank for the maximum time, keeping chatter and vibration problems to a minimum.

True the blank to the finished diameter, then drill a depth hole into the end grain. Hollow the inside, first using a gouge **(A)**, then a round-nose scraper **(B)**. When making identical goblets, work to an internal template **(C)**. Mark the exact depth on the outside of the blank **(D)**, sand the inside **(E)**, then lay out the detail **(F)**.

Turn the bowl profile. Use a parting tool to part in the headstock side of the cup bottom's exterior **(G)**. Initially part in about halfway before using a skew chisel to begin the bowl profile **(H)**. Retain a portion of the left face of the parting cut as a reference point: The bottom of the bowl will be a parting-tool width to the right.

As you near the finished profile, use calipers and a parting tool to establish the diameter of the bead at the top of the stem **(I)**. Then use the skew chisel's long point to complete the bottom of the bowl where it curves into the top of the bead **(J)**. Note that the edge is well clear of the bowl as the point details the top of the bead. Stop the lathe periodically to gauge the wall thickness **(K)**, using a bit of cloth to protect the sanded interior from the caliper jaw.

Now that you're done with the bowl, you can begin work on the stem. First use a gouge to cut back just enough to allow the skew chisel to work **(L)**, then turn the top of the bead with a skew **(M)**. At first, use the skew flat on the rest to peel away the waste on the stem **(N)**, then use the long point down to define the top of the base **(O)**. Finally, shear cut the stem closer to its final diameter **(P)**.

Use a detail gouge for the cove **(Q)** and the skew chisel for planing and cutting into corners **(R, S)**. As the stem thins, support the job behind the cut with your fingers, keeping your thumb on both the rest and tool as a fulcrum.

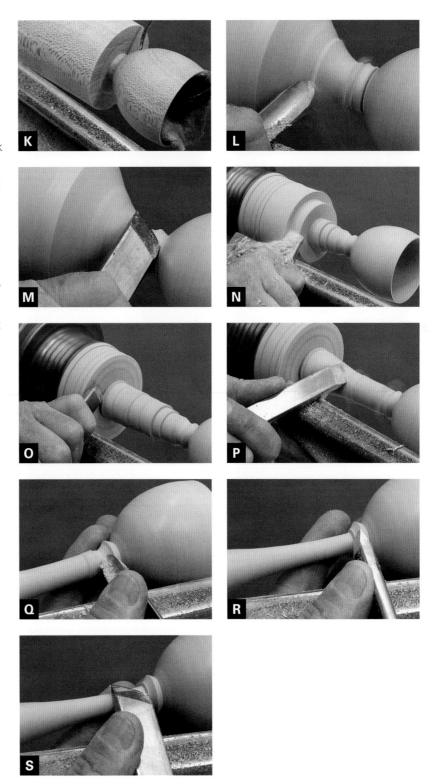

Part in enough to define the base while retaining some mass at the center of the blank **(T)**. Shape the top of the foot with the skew chisel's long point **(U)**. Then sand the bowl, stem, and top of the base with the lathe running **(V)**.

Undercut the base using a parting tool **(W)**, then sand the bottom with abrasive wrapped around a flexible ruler so you can apply pressure in the narrow space **(X)**. Part off with your thumb between the rest and the bowl **(Y)**, lifting the goblet clear as it comes loose **(Z)**. Complete the base by sanding it by hand or against a soft sander **(AA, BB)**.

Box

A turned box is simply a round container with a lid. The top is usually recessed to accept a flange turned on the base. For aesthetic reasons, it's best if the grain lines up at the join. This is not that difficult to do, even though you lose nearly ¾ in. (19mm) at the join. The trick is to divide the top and base sections of the blank at a point where the grain is reasonably straight. **A** shows how the box lies in the blank.

This box, turned from a 3-in.- (75mm-) diameter blank about 6 in. (150mm) long—is mounted in the 50mm shark jaws of my Vicmarc chuck. If your chuck has only smaller jaws, you'll need to turn a short tenon on each end of the blank to fit into your chuck. Then follow the hollowing and fitting directions given here, eventually parting the box lid and bottom from their short tenons.

After turning the blank round, remove the center marks, turning each end slightly concave in the process **(B)**. Part off the base section **(C)** and move the lid blank to the end of the chuck **(D)**. True the face **(E)**, then rough hollow the lid with a gouge.

Now use a square-end scraper to cut a flange at least ½ in. (13mm) long to fit over the base **(F)**. Use calipers to ensure that the sides are parallel **(G)**. Complete the hollowing with scrapers **(H)**, then use a pencil to transfer the exact depth to the outside before sanding and finishing the inside **(I)**. Using a detail gouge, turn as much of the profile as is accessible **(J)**, then remove the lid from the chuck and set it aside for now.

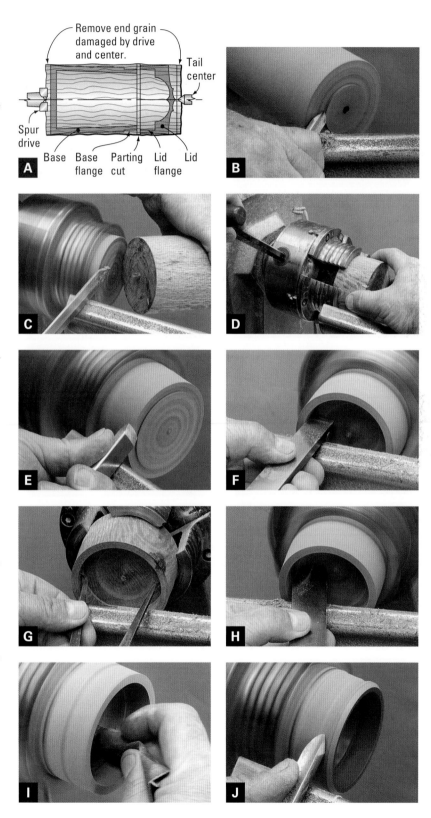

A — Remove end grain damaged by drive and center. Tail center. Spur drive. Base. Base flange. Parting cut. Lid flange. Lid.

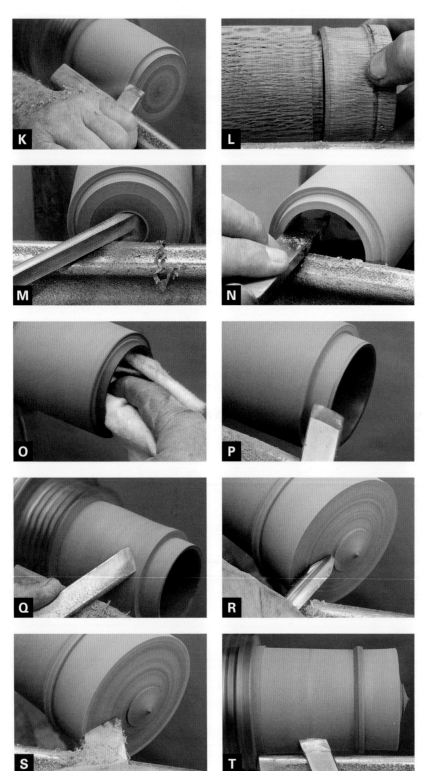

Mount and true the base blank, then turn the very end of the flange to fit the lid **(K)**. The idea at this point is simply to determine the approximate diameter of the flange, which you'll finish cutting after hollowing the base. So turn just enough of the flange to establish that it fits into the lid **(L)**. Drill a depth hole, then hollow the base using gouges and scrapers **(M, N)**. Afterward, sand and finish the inside **(O)**.

Now complete turning the base flange. At this point, you'll want the lid to fit tightly enough to allow you to turn its profile. To gauge the necessary diameter of the flange, hold the lid over it just firmly enough to produce a burnish line from the lid rubbing. Turn down to the burnish mark using the skew chisel flat on its side for a peel/scrape cut **(P)**. Before attaching the lid for its final shaping, use the skew chisel to thin the base wall **(Q)**. With the lid off, the wall thickness is easy to gauge with your fingers.

Jam the lid on, then shape its top using a detail gouge **(R)**. Turn the end and side profile using the skew flat for delicate peel/scrape cuts **(S, T)**.

Leave some roughed beads at the join, making sure that the side profile flows smoothly under the beads. Detail the beads using the skew chisel's long point **(U)**, then sand and polish the profile **(V)**.

[TIP] Incorporate a detail at a join to disguise variations between lid and base.

Now fine-tune the fit of the lid so it's not too difficult to remove. It helps to make the flange slightly domed, leaving the burnished area at the apex of the dome **(W)**. Afterward, polish the flange.

Finally, rechuck the base over a jam chuck **(X)** and use very delicate peeling cuts to turn away the jaw marks **(Y)**. Turn the base slightly concave **(Z)** so it will stand on the rim. Add decoration using a skew flat on its side **(AA)**, then sand and polish. The lid should fit snugly; and when the grain is aligned, the box will look like a solid piece of wood **(BB, CC)**.

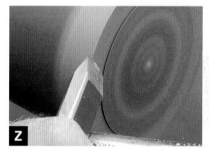

Chasing Threads

Chasing Threads

➤ Chasing Threads by Hand (p. 173)

➤ Chasing Internal Threads (p. 175)

➤ Chasing Threads with a Jig (p. 176)

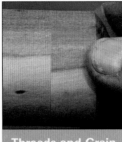

Threads and Grain

➤ Matching a Thread (p. 177)

➤ Achieving Grain Alignment (p. 179)

Threading Project

➤ Condiment Shaker (p. 180)

I N CENTURIES PAST, production turners were constantly cutting, or chasing, threads by hand in order to make best use of valuable hardwoods and ivory. Hand-chasing techniques enabled them to join scraps and off-cuts together, then incorporate them into larger pieces like the baby rattle shown in the photos opposite left. Today studio turners are using hand-chased threads on funeral urns and all manner of smaller containers, like the condiment shaker described later in this section.

Threads can be chased by hand or with a jig. Hand chasers come in pairs. The chaser that cuts outside threads has teeth on the end, while the chaser that cuts inside threads has its teeth on the side. An *armrest* is also very useful, although not essential, to help support the internal chaser in use. Hand chasing is best done at a low lathe speed. A variable-speed control or treadle lathe is almost indispensable, as threads are usually chased on jobs that are otherwise turned at 1800 rpm to 2500 rpm.

A jig makes chasing a thread easy, particularly on a short tenon or a flange that abuts a shoulder, as is typical on a box. However, chasing with a jig is nowhere near as satisfying as hand chasing—or as quick, once you get the hang of the technique. While you

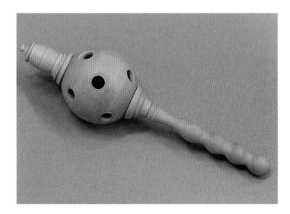

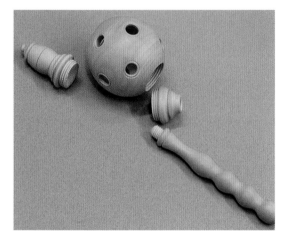

Hand turners often used scraps to manufacture small objects like this boxwood baby rattle made by Bill Jones.

Hand chasing tools come in pairs. The inside chaser is often used with an armrest (*front*). This armrest was fashioned on a high-speed grinder from a ½-in. (13mm) carriage bolt.

A jig, like this Klein threading jig, can cut perfect threads every time.

might start out with a jig, chances are you'll eventually go on to relish the enjoyment of hand chasing.

A certain acknowledgment is due here: Hand-chasing techniques could well have been lost but for the generosity of two English professional turners. Bill Jones and Allan Batty have shared their decades of hand-chasing experience in numerous workshops and symposia, thus reviving interest in this satisfying skill.

Thread Shape and Wood Selection

Old hand-chased threads are often rough and even somewhat loose as they come together. However, when tightened up to a shoulder or bead, the parts firm up so you might never realize that an object is an assembly of several pieces. These days, though, threads are expected to be nearly perfect. The top of a well-made thread should be flat for strength, as seen in drawing A on p. 177. Eventually, however, even well-mated threads will round over with use. Thread sizes are gauged in teeth per inch (tpi), with the most common gauges being 10 tpi, 16 tpi, and 20 tpi.

You don't want threads to splinter or crumble, so dense hardwoods like boxwood, African blackwood, lignum vitae, or gidgee are preferred. However, if you find that the threads on some woods like cocobolo or ebony do chip away, try strengthening them by soaking the section to be chased with thin cyanoacrylate adhesive. There is no guarantee that this will work, but it's worth a go. As an insurance, many turners use cyanoacrylate as a matter of course on all woods.

The grain on the blank should run parallel to the lathe axis. In other words, chasing happens on center work and end-grain projects. Face work and diameters larger than 3 in. (75mm) are rarely chased because there are too many problems with the wood warping and the consequent difficulties screwing components together. Mating threaded surfaces must be cylindrical for a good fit. To ensure a join without gaps, always true the end grain so it is smooth and chamfered slightly inward.

[TIP] Never sand a surface before chasing because the grit that lodges in the wood will dull the cutter edges.

Chasing Threads by Hand

Chasing threads by hand requires a relaxed approach and an ultralight touch. Hold the chasers lightly **(A)**. If you force the tool forward into the cut, you'll tear your thread apart, as you will if you go too slowly. It is essential to move the tool evenly to avoid a distorted or drunken thread. A thread is cut in several passes, with each subsequent pass deepening the thread until it has been cut to full depth.

Run the lathe slowly in the 200-rpm to 600-rpm range. This wide of a range might seem imprecise, but the proper speed depends in part on the diameter you are chasing and in part on the speed at which you feel most comfortable. The most important thing is rhythm; once the thread is started, or struck, let the tool follow the thread without forcing it forward or resisting its advance.

The best way to learn the basics is by cutting an outside thread on a section of blank about ¾ in. (19mm) long and 2½ in. (65mm) or less in diameter—like the largest thread in **(B)**. In reality, most threads are more likely to be short, as on the blank's smallest diameter section. However, in a couple of revolutions, you don't get much time to experience the pace at which the tool travels. Start by chasing a fine thread of 16 tpi or 20 tpi so the tool travels slower than it would when chasing a coarser thread.

Prepare the blank as a trued cylinder with a flat end, then soften the corner to a small radius and make a shallow parting cut, like those to the left of each threaded section in **(B)**. This defines the length of the thread and provides a rebate into which the end of the chaser can travel as you withdraw it. The tool rest must be ultrasmooth so the tool slides along it easily with no hint of resistance. Set the rest so the top of the tool is at center.

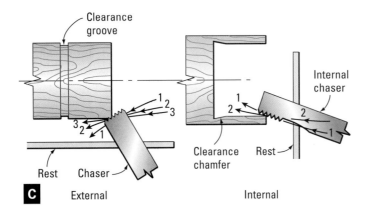

Clearance groove

Internal chaser

Clearance chamfer

Rest

Rest   Chaser

C   External   Internal

The idea is to hold the tool lightly and strike the thread by moving the chaser at an angle across the corner from right to left. Strike the threads at an angle to the lathe axis and take several passes to initiate the thread **(C)**. If you merely push the teeth against the wood, you'll simply cut a set of beads. Before striking the thread, take a few practice passes into space as though preparing a golf putt. Then do it for real, firmly and positively, bringing the teeth up into the cut through a small arc. On subsequent passes, let the chaser teeth drop into the previously cut groove **(B)** and allow the chaser to follow the thread at it own pace. On each pass, bring the tool nearer parallel to the cylinder until you have chased the entire length of the threaded section **(D)**. The slower the lathe is running, the more time you have to watch what's happening.

Once you are cutting the entire length of the thread, put a small amount of pressure toward the axis to deepen the cut **(E)**. Do this by dropping the tool handle slightly, so the teeth pivot into the spiral. Another approach is to ease the tool handle gently to the left as the tool travels along the rest. When the lead tooth reaches the end of the thread, withdraw the tool. Don't cut in so deep that the thread is pointed. The top of the thread needs to be flat for strength.

The threads can be cleaned up by switching the lathe off and rotating the workpiece by hand against the cutter. But a toothbrush actually works better (of course).

D

E

Chasing Internal Threads

Internal threads are cut in much the same way as external threads. The biggest difference is that it's difficult to see what you're doing. So the problem lies in applying just enough pressure to chase the thread as the tool moves in a distorted oval, cutting just above center. A rebate the depth of the thread at the end of the thread makes withdrawing the tool easier at the end of the cut. The thread is struck with the chaser making several passes across the inner lip of the rim before it is brought parallel to the axis (see **C** opposite).

There are two options for supporting the tool. The first is to use the lathe rest, keeping your thumb against the side of the tool blade as a fulcrum **(A)**. Against this, your fingers pull the chaser into the cut on one side, while on the other, your hand pivots the tool clear at the end of the cut.

Alternatively, you can position the rest parallel to the turning axis and use an armrest to pull the chaser into the cut, starting each pass with a slight upward swing of the chasing tool into the cut **(B, C)**. In use, the handle of an armrest is held firmly against your side. Therefore, as it moves along the rest, you need to move with it. This armrest was fashioned by grinding three sides of a long, ½-in. (13mm) carriage bolt back to the square **(D)**.

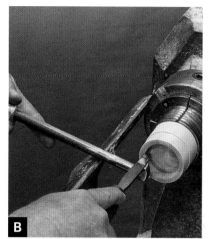

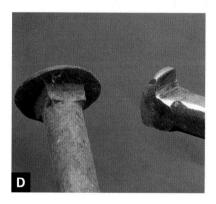

A

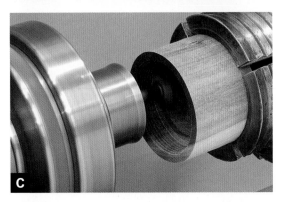
B

C

D

Chasing Threads with a Jig

A jig, like the Klein threading jig shown here, guarantees your ability to chase long, accurate threads free of bends and kinks as well as short threads that terminate against a shoulder. The workpiece is turned on one lathe, then both chuck and workpiece are transferred to the jig, which is usually set up on a small lathe. Alternatively, some turners have a jig set up with the cutter mounted on a small dedicated motor. The thread is cut by winding the workpiece past a cutter running between 2500 rpm and 3000 rpm.

With the chuck on the jig, position the whole assembly so the rim of the cutter is just clear of, but aligned with, the end of the workpiece **(A)**, then lock the jig in position on the lathe. Turn on the cutter, then use the front crank on the jig to wind the workpiece against the tip of the cutter. When you hear the buzz of the cutter making contact with the wood, use the axial crank to wind the workpiece past the cutter to cut the thread. I keep my hand on the chuck to dampen any vibration **(B)**.

The thread is usually cut in a couple passes, although with very little experience it's possible to do it in one **(C)**. Take care not to cut so deep that the top of the thread is sharp, as it will probably break away in use. A magnifying glass is handy for examining the quality of the thread.

An outside thread is cut much the same way, but there is a small problem. When the cutter and workpiece come together, both are rotating in the same downward direction, creating a tendency for the cutter to grab the wood and unwind a small, light chuck before you realize it. To counteract this, I use a heavy chuck, placing my hand on top of it to retard the feed rate and to guard against catches **(D)**.

Matching a Thread

When chasing threads, you can cut either the internal or external thread first. However, general practice is to start with the internal thread. That way, if you have problems with the fit, it's easier to see and correct the mating external threads, which are cut second. I make the inside thread double the length of the outside thread, which needs only a couple of spirals to be user friendly. A lid that takes more than two rotations to lock down is tedious to use (no matter how much you enjoy chasing the threads).

Invariably, the two threaded portions of an object need to screw together tightly. For this to happen, you must first ensure that the ends coming together are turned true and that there is a clearance space either at the start of the inside thread or the end of the outside thread. This space can be cut as a shallow rebate, but I find a chamfer sufficient and less intrusive aesthetically **(A)**. Be sure to make the inside thread (on the lid) longer. On a box, you don't need more than two spirals on the base.

After you have chased an inside thread, chamfer the end of the thread using the side of a skew chisel bevel **(B)**. Make the chamfer 45 degrees, so the thread starts halfway up the slope. On a box lid, sand and finish the inside **(C)**, then brush the thread clear of dust **(D)**.

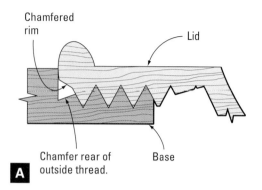

Chamfered rim

Lid

Chamfer rear of outside thread.

Base

A

B

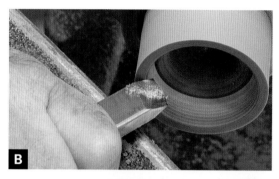

C

D

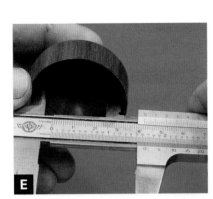

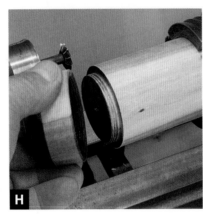

When the inside thread is completed, set your Vernier calipers to the diameter **(E)**. The diameter of the outside thread will need to be slightly larger than that diameter for the threads to interlock. For this 16-tpi thread, I expanded the caliper jaws a shade less than ⅟₁₆ in. (2mm) to set the diameter for the outside thread **(F)**. Err on the side of caution, making the diameter larger rather than smaller. You can always cut the thread a bit deeper, whereas you cannot replace what you've chased away.

Cut the thread **(G)**, then wind the jig clear of the cutter to test the fit **(H)**. Do not unlock the jig to test the fit, as it is difficult to relocate it in exactly the same position. If the parts don't fit together or if they're stiff, take another light cut. When the parts screw together nicely, transfer the chuck back to the turning lathe and complete the turning.

Achieving Grain Alignment

If there is any sort of character to the wood, as there is on this quaintly named piece of Australian dead finish (*Acacia tetragonophylla*), it's nice to align the grain on the top and the base so the pattern flows uninterrupted through the join when the lid's screwed on tight.

First you need to determine how far off the alignment is. Screw the lid on tight, then back it off until the grain aligns. If the grain isn't distinct enough to serve as an obvious reference, draw a pencil line across the join.

Here the grain is about half a turn off matching **(A)**. In addition, there is a gap created by cutting a tad too far with the threading jig, which is easy to do. However, this is not a problem as the shoulder invariably needs reducing to match the grain. Use the side of a skew chisel bevel to reduce the shoulder by about half a thread's width **(B)** so the lid can go that extra half turn.

Actually, it pays to leave the grain just short of alignment **(C)** because threads and rims ease slightly with use. If you align the grain perfectly at this point **(D)**, chances are you'll end up with a mismatch almost as soon as the job is finished **(E)**.

At this stage on a box, use a skew chisel's long point to cut a small V-groove on the join. This chamfers the outer lip of each rim and removes the very sharp edges. It also brings the parts nearer alignment in the finished piece **(F)**. In this situation, the shoulder needed to be reduced by three-quarters of a thread width to bring the grain into alignment.

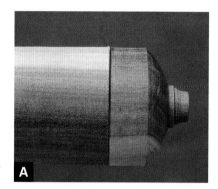

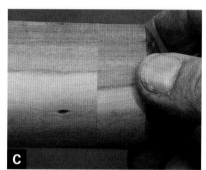
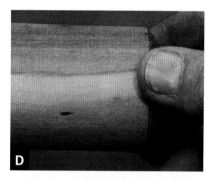
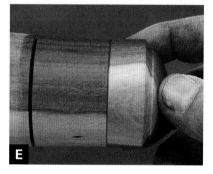
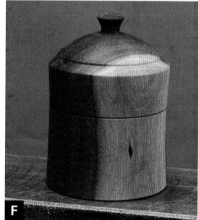

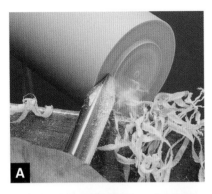

Condiment Shaker

Salt and pepper shakers are usually drilled out, then plugged with a rubber bung, which is often difficult to remove and insert when you need to refill the container. A screw top makes more sense and you can create a bigger interior space by turning. This 1⅝-in.- (42mm-) diameter, 4-in.- (100mm-) tall boxwood shaker sports a bead between the lid and base to make the join less obvious. Inside, the top of the lid beyond and above the flange widens to make chasing easier and the lid thinner. To make your shaker, use a dense hardwood held in long chuck jaws to provide maximum support, particularly when hollowing the base.

After you've trued the blank and before you part off the bulk for the base, turn the end slightly concave (**A**). This will be the bottom of the shaker, and it pays to turn it now because it's really a nasty job later when it's jammed on a chuck. Part off the base section (**B**).

Hollow the lid (**C**), ensuring that the flange is cylindrical. Chase the thread in the lid either by hand (**D**) or on a jig, then use the bevel side of a skew chisel to chamfer the inner lip of the rim (**E**). On a typical box, I would apply finish to a lid at this point; however, with this sort of container I don't, because I want the wood to absorb the aroma of the contents.

While the lid is gripped firmly in the chuck, turn as much of the outside as you can with a small, ⅜-in. (9mm) detail gouge (**F, G**). Measure the inside diameter of the lid **(H)**, then widen the caliper jaws for gauging the diameter of the base flange. I'm using 16-tpi chasers here so I widened the jaws about ¹⁄₁₆ in. (1.8mm).

Establish the diameter of the base flange **(I)** keeping it short, maintaining as much bulk as possible in the blank while it's hollowed. Next, hollow the base using scrapers **(J)**. Mark the depth on the tool blade so you don't go through the bottom.

With the inside completed, prepare for threading by extending the flange to about ½ in. (13mm) long, using a skew chisel or a wide parting tool. Then ease in the corner of the skew at the base of the flange to create a clearance chamfer **(K)** (see **A** on p. 177). If, when you come to turn the flange, you find that the blank shifted off center during hollowing, try to relocate it accurately in the chuck. If you can't, then cut off the flange and turn another that runs true.

Chase the base flange **(L)** and check the lid fit **(M)**. Before aligning the grain, finish shaping as much of the base as possible **(N)**. With the lid off, you'll be able to check the wall thickness quickly with your fingers.

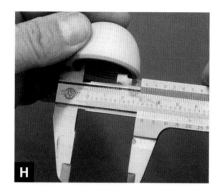

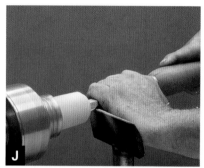

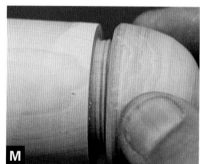

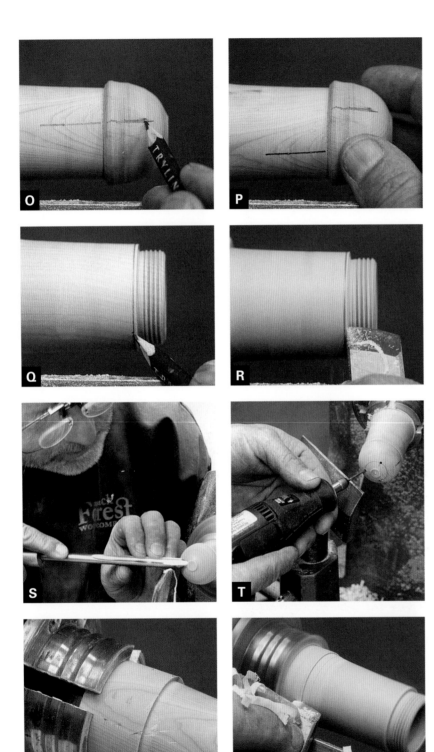

Now screw the lid on, line up the grain, and draw a reference line across the two portions **(O)**. Tighten the lid so you can assess how much of the flange shoulder to remove to bring the grain into alignment **(P)**. Here it is almost a whole turn, so I mark almost the width of the thread on the shoulder **(Q)** and use the side of the skew chisel bevel to turn back to that line, keeping the shoulder flat **(R)**.

When the grain is almost aligned, screw the lid on and finish shaping it **(S)**. When turning fine detail like this, I use 3X magnifiers that clip over my spectacles. Their depth of field requires getting very close to the action. Although it's uncomfortable bending over the lathe so near an object that could explode in the event of a catch, at least I can see what I'm doing.

Once the lid is turned, mark a circle on which to lay out the holes. This shaker was always destined to hold the ground pepper I use for cooking, so I drilled three holes using a Dremel grinder **(T)**. After drilling the holes, sand the whole profile, but polish only the lid.

Finishing the lower portion of the base over a jam chuck is difficult because of the ever-present possibility of catches ruining the job. Therefore, the more work you can do in the mechanical chuck the better. Shift the blank in the jaws so it's gripped by the very end **(U)** and use peeling cuts with the skew chisel to shape all the way to the chuck jaws **(V)**.

Reverse the workpiece over a jam chuck **(W)**. Use your left hand to serve as tail-center support while the thumb stays in contact with the tool on the rest **(X)**.

It's safer is to use tail-center support with the job pressed against a protective block that is as wide as the rim of the base. Turn away the surplus with a ⅜-in. (9mm) shallow gouge, working into the protective block as need be **(Y)**, then gently use the skew chisel to peel away the remainder of the waste **(Z)**.

Finally, turn a small chamfer on the rim of the base, using the skew chisel's long point **(AA)**. If you failed to turn the base at the beginning, it now needs to be dished very slightly so the shaker sits on the rim only. Use your left hand to keep the job running true and a ⅜-in. (9mm) shallow gouge to make a very light cut to center **(BB, CC)**.

W

X

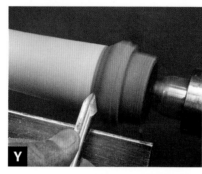

Y

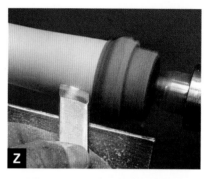

Z

AA

BB

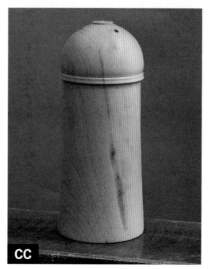

CC

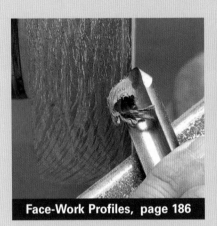

Face-Work Profiles, page 186

Face-Work Hollowing, page 207

PART FIVE

Face Work

ALTHOUGH THE TERM FACE WORK typically applies to bowls and platters, it actually refers to any job in which the grain on the piece being turned is oriented perpendicular to the lathe axis. Blanks are typically mounted on a faceplate or chuck, usually without tail-center support, so it's possible to present the tools from all angles.

Face work presents a greater variety of grain than center work, so you need a wider range of tools. This is especially true if you want to turn beads and coves, which demand different techniques, depending on whether they are on a face or a side. Shallow and detailing gouges are used to cut detail on profiles. However, the main tools are long and strong deep-fluted bowl gouges and scrapers used for rough hollowing and smoothing surfaces.

Face-work catches are more dangerous than center-work catches, so you should always wear face protection against the inevitable disintegrating blank.

Face-Work Profiles

Face-Work Techniques

➤ Truing and Roughing Cuts (p. 190)

➤ Truing Faces and Cylinders (p. 191)

➤ Finishing Cuts Using Gouges (p. 191)

➤ Using Scrapers on Profiles (p. 192)

Face-Work Details

➤ Cutting into a Corner (p. 194)

➤ Grooves (p. 194)

➤ Beads on a Side (p. 195)

➤ Beads on a Face (p. 196)

➤ Coves (p. 198)

Face-Work Projects

➤ Trophy Base (p. 199)

➤ Frame (p. 201)

➤ Stool (p. 204)

ON FACE WORK, THE GRAIN runs at 90 degrees to the lathe axis. Therefore, on face-work profiles, all cuts are made from smaller to larger diameter, so as each fiber is cut, it is supported by fibers behind it. Be sure to always cut in from a face to prevent the edge from splitting.

On profiles, use gouges to do the bulk of the work and keep scrapers for refining gouge-cut surfaces, delicate finishing cuts, and detailing. Don't use scrapers for heavy roughing cuts on profiles; gouges are faster and less brutal. For all my face work, I use mostly ½-in. (13mm) and ⅜-in. (9mm) gouges with rounded wings on the tool edge that cut nice fat shavings. Larger tools don't

enable me to remove waste any faster. Never use skew chisels for face work; they are designed to shear grain lying parallel to the lathe axis only.

If the cutting portion of the edge lies at about 45 degrees to the on-coming wood, it will shear cut the wood cleanly. The edge must be supported by the bevel or lie in line with the fulcrum (where the tool contacts the rest). When the bevel isn't rubbing the wood, a gouge must be used on its side—never with the flute up. If you use a shallow gouge flute up for face work, it will *always* catch.

There are broadly two ways of using a gouge to shear cut. For roughing cuts, the gouge is used pointing up into the on-coming wood with the handle lying at near

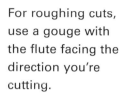

FACE-WORK SHEAR CUTS

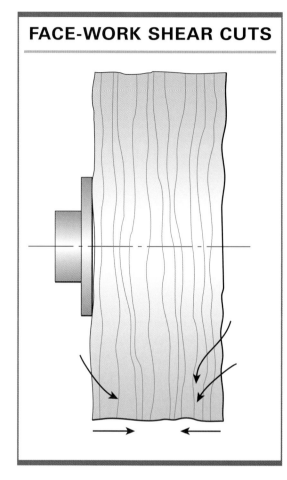

For roughing cuts, use a gouge with the flute facing the direction you're cutting.

90 degrees to the lathe axis. The bevel doesn't contact the wood as the gouge is pulled into the cut going from right to left or pushed from left to right. In each case, the gouge is rolled over about 45 degrees, with the flute facing the direction of the gouge travel. The cleanest cut, used for finishing cuts, is made with the bevel rubbing the wood with the tool near horizontal and pointing in the direction you are cutting.

When you're turning a profile, the rest can usually be positioned close to the surface being cut. You don't need the strength of deep-fluted bowl gouges designed for hollowing well over the rest. I use a bowl gouge on a profile only when the gouge is too short for hollowing. I prefer to use less-expensive

The cleanest cut is made with the bevel rubbing, and with the tool near horizontal and pointing in the direction you are cutting.

Lathe Speeds for Even-Grained Face-Work Blanks

Speeds are shown in revolutions per minute (rpm). The exact speed at which a blank can be spun safely depends on its density and balance. Blanks with uneven grain and density should be started at half these speeds. Always err on the side of caution, starting from near 0 rpm if you have a variable-speed lathe.

| | **THICKNESS** | | | | |
DIAMETER	**2" (50mm)**	**3"(75mm)**	**4"(100mm)**	**5"(125mm)**	**6"(150mm)**
4" (100mm)	1800	1600	1500	1400	1300
6" (150mm)	1600	1500	1400	1300	1100
8" (200mm)	1500	1400	1300	1100	900
10" (255mm)	1400	1300	1100	900	800
12" (305mm)	1300	1100	900	800	700
14" (355mm)	1100	900	800	600	500
16" (410mm)	900	800	600	500	400

▶ CUTTING A CHUCK REBATE

Modern chucks enable you to mount jobs over expanding jaws that sit in a shallow dovetailed rebate. To cut the rebate, use a ½-in. (13mm) skewed scraper with a left corner of about 87 degrees. The scraper is also sharpened on its side, and the front edge should be slightly radiused. Use only a small portion of the edge at one time, swinging the tool sideways on the rest to cut the bottom of the rebate flat.

shallow gouges because their open flutes never jam with shavings—a problem with deep-fluted gouges, particularly when turning green wood.

Cutting Face-Work Details

Cutting beads, coves, grooves, and other details on a thin wall is dangerous, particularly near the rim of an out-flowing bowl that is already hollowed. Any tool pressure against the wood causes it to flex and catch the edge. Catches are severe, and a disintegrating bowl or vase can cause serious injury.

Gouges are safer to use than scrapers. Ideally, decoration should be turned before a form is hollowed or, if you are working with a roughed form, before the wall gets too thin and flexible. On a bowl up to 6 in. (150mm) in diameter, the wall thickness should be at least ½ in. (13mm). On a 12-in.-(305mm-) diameter bowl, the wall should be at least

1 in. (25mm) thick. If a roughed bowl is mounted over a large jaw, as shown in photo A on p. 78, there should be sufficient support for the bowl wall for you to cut in beads, coves, or grooves without the tool grabbing.

Face-Work Profile Projects

The projects in this section will give you the opportunity to put to use several face-work techniques.

Trophy bases and similar bases for figurines are bread-and-butter projects for many professional turners. Over the one shown here, I fit a glass dome, the sort you put over something delicate or simply difficult to dust.

A frame is an attractive, utilitarian project that can be used to display photos or to mount a mirror. And it can be made from rings cut as you rough turn large bowls.

The stool is a piece of furniture every child should have the moment he can struggle to his feet. It's small, and I call it an heirloom stool. Very small children can use it as a table and climbing aid, after which it becomes a seat. As adults, they'll find it handy as a low table or a footstool. Make it well, and your stool can pass from generation to generation, as has a square version in my family. The legs on this stool are angled so the feet splay outward for stability. The type of leg you choose to turn is up to you. However your tastes run, turn one leg, then copy it.

▶ BEVELING AN ARRIS

A sharp edge or arris on wood can cut flesh, especially when spinning on the lathe. As well as being dangerous, sharp rims break and splinter easily. And they don't feel comfortable on a finished object. For all these reasons, it's good practice to soften sharp edges with a small bevel, not just for your personal safety when turning, but also for the aesthetics of your work. Use a shear scraper or spear-point scraper on edge to soften corners.

Truing and Roughing Cuts

When roughing, the idea is to arrive at a slightly oversize version of what you want as quickly and efficiently as possible. Blanks with even grain will mostly spin true with minimal vibration. Therefore, on rounded forms, don't bother to true the side to a cylinder first. Instead, simply remove the bulk of the waste from corners to reduce any vibration as quickly as possible.

Surface quality is not of primary importance at the roughing stage, so don't worry about the tool bevel rubbing. Start the gouge near horizontal on its side with the flute facing the wood, then rotate the lower edge into the wood as you drop the handle. When the edge is at about 45 degrees to the oncoming wood, it will slice a curly shaving rather than tear and scrape **(A)**.

Make a series of sweeping cuts with the lower wing of the gouge **(B)**, taking the edge through an arc into and through the wood and on into space. Try not to push the tool against the wood; rather let the wood come to the tool.

Truing Faces and Cylinders

It is a good habit to true any face, unless you want to retain the uneven surface. The main benefit is reducing vibration so you can spin the wood faster, but truing also reduces a blank to its useable, defect-free dimensions.

Take a series of small cuts into the face starting at the rim. Keep your hand firmly on the rest and squeeze the edge into the wood with your fingers **(A)**, ceasing each cut when the *tick-tick* noise stops. Use the lower edge of the gouge to true the surface **(B)**. When the worst of the unevenness is removed, roll the tool over so the bevel rubs and take a shear cut to the center **(C)**. Mirror these cuts to true the headstock face **(D)**. Note that for this cut, the shaving comes off the wing of the edge, whereas when truing a side **(E)**, the shaving is just below the nose of the gouge.

True a cylindrical blank by cutting in from either face **(E, F)**. With the tool near horizontal, keep the bevel rubbing. Use the lower edge of a deep-fluted gouge or the nose of a shallow gouge.

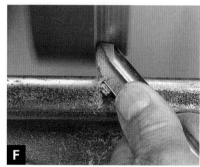
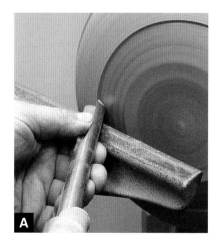

Finishing Cuts Using Gouges

Either deep-fluted or shallow gouges can be used to make a finishing shear cut. Keep the tool near horizontal and pointing in the direction you're cutting **(A)**. Start with the gouge on its side, then roll the tool to about 45 degrees for the best shaving. Cut with the nose of the tool and keep the bevel rubbing the wood at all times **(B)**. As the cut proceeds, keep your weight behind the tool, the bevel rubbing, and the tool near horizontal.

Using Scrapers on Profiles

Scrapers are mostly used flat on the rest with the blades tilted down slightly. That way, if they catch they swing into space. Most gouge-cut surfaces can be improved by some sort of scraping technique if you go gently enough. Tool pressure against the wood should be similar to the amount of pressure you use to rub your hands under a hot-air hand dryer. You wouldn't push your hands together so hard so that you can't rub them.

Scrapers should stroke the wood. This is easiest to do by using slightly skewed scrapers, which you can drag at an angle to the surface you're cutting. On a flat face, you can use some pressure and take ribbon shavings **(A)** as you sweep the tool along the rest. On a side, where you encounter two areas of end grain, go more gently, producing only dust or very small curly shavings **(B)**.

[TIP] **If you see an area of torn end grain, always check the opposite side of the workpiece, as that end grain is usually torn, too.**

In either of these situations, you can also tilt the tool on its side to present the lower half of the edge at about 45 degrees to the on-coming wood for a shear scrape **(C)**. On a face, pull the tool away from the center. On a side, work the tool from the smaller to the larger diameter in a series of small sweeps, using no more than ¼ in. (6mm) of the edge at a time. Curves on the headstock side will need a right-skew scraper.

Skewed scrapers with acute points enable you to work into corners at the base of beads **(D, E)**. To shear scrape into a corner, you need a spear-point scraper. Start the cut in the corner with the tool on its side and pitched up about 10 degrees from horizontal **(F)**. Then simply drop the handle so the edge strokes the surface in a small arc, after which you can pull the tool back along the rest.

A half-cove can be shear scraped using a round-nose scraper on edge **(G)**.

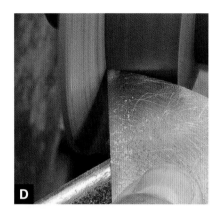

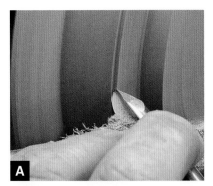

A

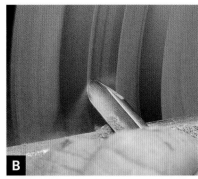

B

C

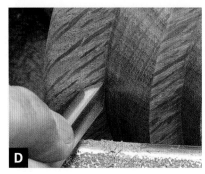

D

Cutting into a Corner

There are many occasions when you need to cut into a corner at the top of a foot, the base of a bead, or under a rim. For this, use a shallow or detail gouge with a long fingernail grind. Start with the gouge on its side **(A)**, then roll it slightly clockwise for a better shaving **(B)** before bringing it back on its side so only the nose is in the corner **(C)**. When you have to cut against the grain (which is quite often), move the tool forward very slowly, again finishing with the gouge on its side so you don't catch either wing **(D)**.

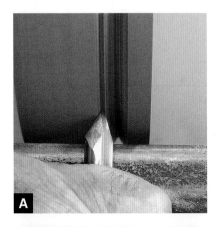

A

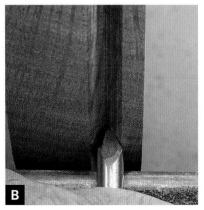

B

C

Grooves

Grooves are best cut using a long-beveled, fingernail-ground detail gouge that can slice cleanly across the fibers. Start the gouge on its side with the handle dropped about 45 degrees below horizontal. Pivot the edge into the wood from one side **(A)**, then the other **(B)**.

Grooves can also be cut using a spear-point scraper **(C)**, but be warned that a heavy catch and severely torn grain are the price of a slightly heavy hand. Start with the point pitched down and pivot it up through an arc into the wood by dropping the handle.

Beads on a Side

Beads on a side are left roughed as a block while the surface beneath is completed and shear cut against the base of the bead.

Using a long-beveled, fingernail-ground detail gouge, start cutting with the gouge on its side **(A)**. Then drop the handle, simultaneously rolling the tool slightly clockwise for a shear cut **(B)**. At the top of the bead, pivot the point back into the wood, rolling the tool back onto its side as you bring the handle back to horizontal **(C)**. Your right hand (on the handle) moves in a counterclockwise vertical oval.

If you are turning a pair or more of beads, pivot the tool on its point so the blade moves along the rest **(D)**. Then repeat the rolling action to cut the next bead **(E)**. At the other end of the pair or row, mirror the first cut **(F)**. Any facets can be shear scraped using a spear-point scraper **(G)**.

Inset beads are turned the same way after making an initial cut to pivot the nose of the gouge into the wood.

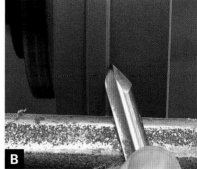
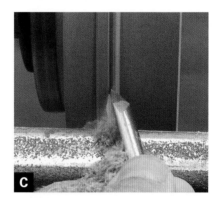
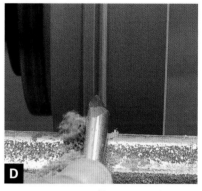

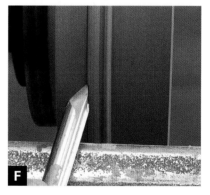

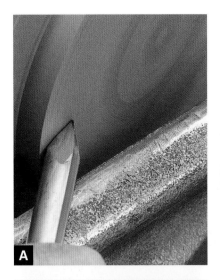

Beads on a Face

Beads on a face are shear cut from the top with a long-beveled, fingernail-ground detail gouge. Beads can be either inset or standing.

To cut inset beads on a face, start the tool on its side (**A**) and pivot the nose into the wood (**B**). Next, cut from the other direction to create the left side of the bead (**C**). Then imitate the first cut, pivoting the nose into the wood over the groove to turn the right side of the bead (**D, E**).

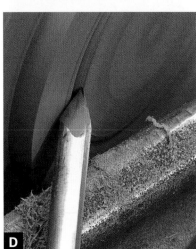

Finally, clean up the right shoulder of the new groove to define the bead or start another bead **(F, G)**.

Standing beads are left roughed out while the surface below is turned. Afterward, cut from the top of the bead to either side **(H, I, J)**. At the end of the cut, the gouge must be on its side with the bevel rubbing the bead. The gouge pivots on the rest, with the handle moving through an arc on a diagonal. Any facets can be shear scraped with a spear-point scraper **(K)**.

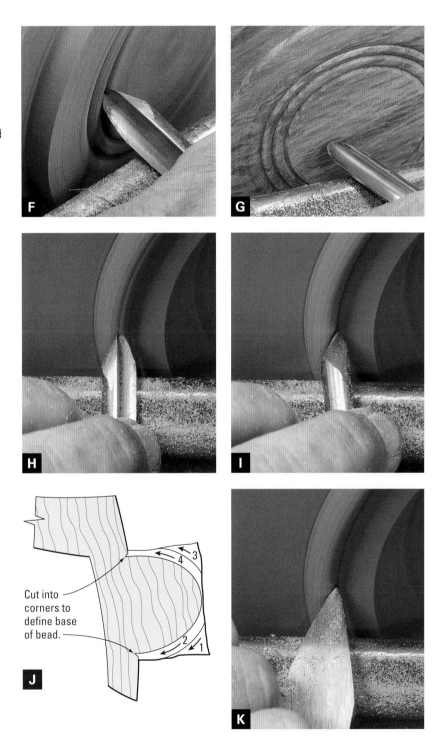

Cut into corners to define base of bead.

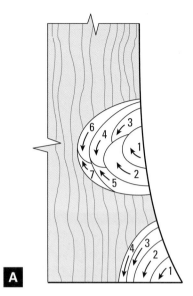

Coves

A cove is cut with a steep-beveled gouge working in from either side **(A)**. Start with the gouge on its side and the handle about 45 degrees below horizontal. Cut in from either side, gradually rolling the tool until it's about 45 degrees at the bottom of the cove **(B)**.

Alternatively, use no more than a small section of a round-nose scraper to make the same series of cuts **(C)**. Swing the handle from one side to the other to keep the rest of the edge clear of a catch.

A half cove can always be shear cut with the grain. Start the gouge on its side with your hand planted on the rest **(D)** and squeeze the edge through an arc **(E)**.

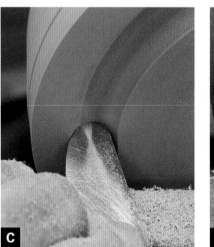

Trophy Base

The wood for this project should be well seasoned and known for its stability, like mahogany or this forest she-oak (*Casuarina*). This 1½-in.-(40mm-) thick base is 5¾ in. (145mm) in diameter, with a groove in the top to accept a 4-in.-(100mm-) diameter glass dome. The dome will need to be slightly loose in the groove to allow for some wood shrinkage.

Blanks for production are typically planed and sanded on one face, then that face is mounted against a screw chuck. That's the approach I took here. The advantage to this method is that the job need be fixed on the lathe only once. The disadvantage is that it leaves a screw hole in the underside, which needs to be plugged to complete the job.

To avoid plugs, you'll need to initially grab the blank in some large jaws while you turn the base and a chuck rebate. Then you'll remount the base on the chuck rebate for turning the opposite face. Another alternative to using a screw chuck is to fix the blank to a waste block on a faceplate using hot glue or double-sided tape; but for either of these, the face against the faceplate needs to be flat.

Here the blank was flattened on a belt sander and mounted on a screw chuck. After you've flattened the top face with a gouge, lay out the diameter and the location of the groove for the dome **(A)**. To cut the ¼-in.- (6mm-) deep groove, use a thin parting tool whose width is about one and a half times the thickness of the dome rim **(B)**.

Turn the blank down to the correct diameter and rough out the cove using a gouge **(C)**.

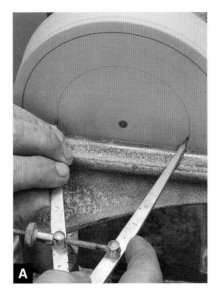

D

E

Then cut the beads at either end of the cove with a ⅜-in. (9mm) detail gouge **(D)**. Use a radiused scraper with a sharp right corner to smooth the cove between the beads **(E)**.

I decided another line was needed to balance the first on the vertical side, and used the small gouge again **(F)**.

F

Frame

This 16-in.- (400mm-) diameter jarrah (*Eucalyptus marginata*) burl frame holds a 12¹³⁄₁₆-in. (300mm) mirror backed by a disc made of hardboard (such as Masonite.) The front and profile (side) of the mirror are completed keeping at least ¾ in. (19mm) thickness for the back in which to fix the mirror and its retaining disc. Then the workpiece is remounted so the two rebates can be turned into the back. One rebate is equal to the thickness of the mirror or picture you're framing; the other is for the backing disc, which is held in place by four screws, and can be deeper **(A)**.

Frame blanks can be rings. When roughing large wide-rimmed bowls, I use a slicer (see photo on p. 20) to cut rings from around a base **(B)**. Afterward, the rings are set aside for seasoning **(C)**. Alternatively, you could cut several of diminishing size from one seasoned disc using a slicer **(B)**. Don't use a high-speed steel (HSS) parting tool, as these can break if you have a catch. The tool needs to be of softer and stronger carbon steel.

Mount the ring over a chuck. Here, I used 5½-in. (140mm) Vicmarc multipurpose jaws, which can expand to 9¼ in. (235mm). Alternatively, you could use wooden jam chucks throughout this project (see drawing A on p. 79). Begin by truing the face (the front of the frame), then the side **(D)**. That way, if the blank isn't secure you can reverse it on to bowl jaws, turn the central rim true for more secure chuck mounting, then return to the original fixing.

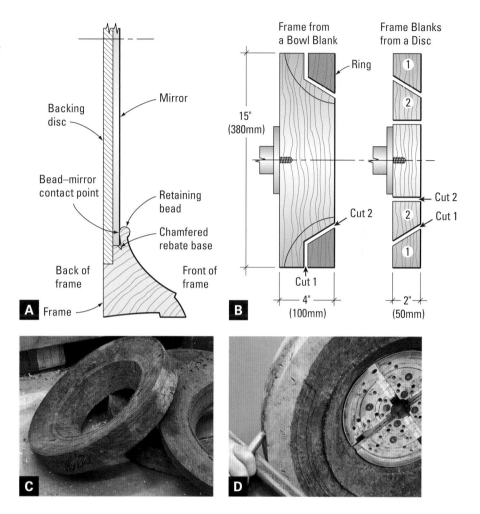

A Frame

Mirror

Backing disc

Bead–mirror contact point

Retaining bead

Chamfered rebate base

Back of frame

Front of frame

B

Frame from a Bowl Blank

Frame Blanks from a Disc

Ring

15" (380mm)

4" (100mm)

2" (50mm)

Cut 1

Cut 2

Cut 1

Cut 2

1

2

1

2

1

C

D

Lay out the mirror diameter less ¾ in. (19mm) **(E)**, then use a square-end scraper to cut a series of steps as you work toward the line **(F)**. Keep all cuts parallel to the lathe axis; if you widen the marked diameter, the opening might be too big to retain the mirror. Don't worry if you cut it undersize because it will be easy to enlarge from the other side when the workpiece is rechucked. With the chuck in the center of the blank, it's impossible to cut all the way through, but cut as close as you dare to the chuck jaws.

With the inside diameter set, begin to shape the front of the frame and roughly shape the outside profile **(G)** before refining the form. Behind the retaining bead on the inner lip of the frame, the wood needs to be at least ¾ in. (19mm) thick to accommodate the two rebates on the back (you'll need more if you are framing something thicker than a mirror). Sand the front and profile, then reverse the frame, gripping it by the rim in bowl jaws or a jam chuck **(H)**. True the face, then lay out the diameter of the mirror rebate **(I)**.

Now widen the central hole until you meet the inner lip of the retaining bead. Here there is a lot to remove, so I use a spear-point scraper to cut through to the other side, saving another ring **(J)**. Use the same tool to round over the inner lip of the retaining bead, which is the inside of the frame.

Next cut the rebate for the mirror **(K)**. Use a skewed scraper so you can chamfer the bottom into the corner, allowing the mirror to seat against only the rim of the opening. Then turn the backing disc rebate so it is flat and level with the back of the mirror. Check for flatness using a short straightedge **(L)**. You will not see light beneath either end of the rule if the rebate is flat.

Finally, you need a means of hanging the mirror. You can purchase brass inserts, but a 1¼-in. (30mm) washer pinned over a hole works fine **(M)**. Drill the washer rebate first so the washer sits flush with the frame surface, then drill a smaller, deeper hole that will accommodate a large nail head or picture hook **(N)**.

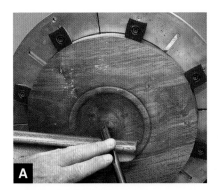

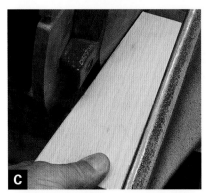

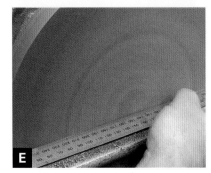

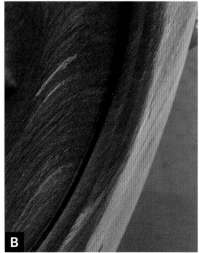

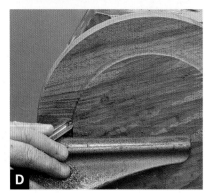

Stool

The blanks for this stool are an 11-in.- (280mm-) diameter disc and three 2-in. (50mm) squares 9 in. (230mm) long. The disc for the seat is initially mounted in bowl jaws so a rebate can be turned for an expanding chuck in what will be the base **(A)**.

The seat can also be turned on one fixing. In that case, you plane or sand the disc on the face that will be the underside, drill a hole at the center, and mount the blank on a screw chuck. The downside is that this leaves a hole to be plugged.

Alternatively, you can glue a waste block to what will be the stool top, and then mount the waste blank to a screw chuck or faceplate, so you can turn the rebate. Afterward, you turn away the waste block. Chucks speed the process enormously, but they leave obvious chuck marks, which I try to disguise with decorative detail. Here 4-in. (100mm) jaws will expand into this small ⅛-in.- (3mm) deep groove **(B)** located beneath the bead that decorates the rim of the rebate. You can make it as fancy or simple as your mood and nerve take you.

A 15-degree chamfer on the underside of the seat allows the leg tenons to intersect the surface at 90 degrees for a stronger joint. It also gives the stool seat a lighter look when viewed from above. To establish the angle of the chamfer, set the tool rest at 90 degrees to the lathe bed, then use the rest as a base for an angle gauge **(C)**. As you turn the chamfer, check it occasionally with the gauge. The chamfer can also be turned once the seat is rechucked in preparation for turning the top.

The top of the seat needs to be flat before the holes are drilled for the legs. After remounting the seat on the expanding chuck, turn the top flat with a gouge **(D)**. Check the surface by holding a straightedge against the spinning wood **(E)**. Then flatten the burnished high spots by gently shear scraping the dark lines away. Test with the rule again and, when the surface seems flat, sand it with a block with the lathe running.

Lay out the leg positions by marking a line about 1¾ in. (45mm) in from the edge **(F)**. Then remove the seat from the lathe and use the radius to the pencil line to locate the three positions for the legs by measuring off around the circle. First set dividers to the radius **(G)**, pushing the divider point into the pencil line to mark the position of one leg. This first leg location should lie on grain that passes through the center of the seat. Then, beginning at that point, walk the dividers around the circle **(H)**, pressing the point into the line on every other step to mark the remaining leg centers **(I)**. You should end up exactly where you started.

The leg holes need to be drilled at 90 degrees to the chamfered surface that you turned on the underside of the seat. If your drill-press table doesn't tilt, clamp a jig to the table at a 15-degree angle, then set the drill so its rim stops ⅛ in. (3mm) short of the jig surface **(J)**. The jig is simply a tilted board with two pins equidistant from a central line to support the seat. The centerline must be aligned with the center spur of the drill **(K, L)**. The holes are 1¾ in. (45mm) in diameter.

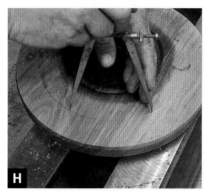

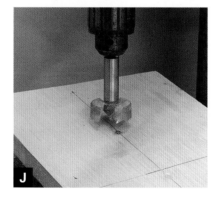

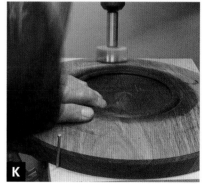

M

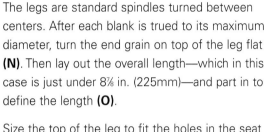

N

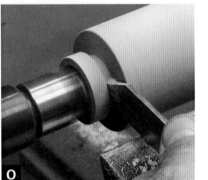

O

P

Q

R

Remount the seat on the lathe to cut any details in the side **(M)**, then sand and finish the seat. Do not get finish in the drill holes.

The legs are standard spindles turned between centers. After each blank is trued to its maximum diameter, turn the end grain on top of the leg flat **(N)**. Then lay out the overall length—which in this case is just under 8⅞ in. (225mm)—and part in to define the length **(O)**.

Size the top of the leg to fit the holes in the seat using a template **(P)**. Make the template by drilling a hole in some scrap, using the same drill you used for the holes in the seat, then cut this in half. The tops of these legs are 1¾ in. (45mm) in diameter, turned to fit holes the same size. Test-fit each leg before you complete the turning. At its thinnest, each leg is 1⅜ in. (35mm) in diameter, flaring out to 2 in. (50mm), which is the maximum diameter of the blank.

After gluing the legs in place, set the stool on a flat surface and mark where they need to be cut so the bottom ends will sit flat on the floor **(Q, R)**.

Face-Work Hollowing

Hollowing Face Work

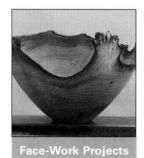

Face-Work Projects

THE TOOLS AND CUTS USED for hollowing face work are much the same as those for shaping a profile, except that now all cuts go from the rim to the base. Hollowing a bowl—the archetypal face-work project—provides some of woodturning's most exhilarating moments, as thick shavings arc from the tool into spongy piles on the bench and floor.

The tools for hollowing face work are primarily the long and strong, deep-fluted bowl gouges. When turning diameters up to 4 in. (100mm) when the depth is less than 3 in. (75mm), a ³⁄₈-in. (9mm) gouge will be strong enough. Projects with larger diameters and more depth require the greater mass of a ¹⁄₂-in. (13mm) deep-fluted gouge.

For most hollowing, I find that a ¹⁄₂-in. (13mm) gouge is ideal for bowls up to 5 in. (125mm) high, which is about as tall as a practical dinner-table bowl needs to be. For depths greater than 6 in. (150mm), scrapers are often a better option for rough hollowing and much less expensive than gouges.

To shear cut, all cuts are made from larger to smaller diameter. Using either gouges or scrapers, aim your cuts as much as possible toward the area of the chuck rather than directing the pressure against the axis.

The most difficult areas to cut cleanly are the two sections of end grain on opposite sides of a blank. This is particularly a problem when undercutting rims on enclosed forms. You'll usually get best results from a

For many people, creating piles of spongy shavings is the main attraction of turning wood. These go into gardens as mulch.

CUTS FOR HOLLOWING FACE WORK

Depth hole

Face cut

gouge, although occasionally a sharp corner on a scraper can be used effectively. Whichever the tool, don't rush its edge into the cut, especially when traveling parallel to or away from the lathe axis. Go slowly, waiting longer than usual for the wood to come to the tool.

Before hollowing with either gouges or scrapers, first drill a depth hole. This will save you a lot of stopping and starting and measuring. When cutting, try to keep a tool moving toward the center of the base, cutting as near parallel to the axis as possible so any force is directed within the diameter of the chuck jaws holding the job.

When you've practiced the techniques shown in the first four projects in this section, you may want to try your hand at making some of the pieces shown in the last five. Each of these projects is hollowed into some form of bowl.

The straight-sided, flat-bottomed sushi tray is an excellent exercise for scrapers. Although the tray bottom can be slightly domed for additional strength, those who

cannot contemplate the thought of raw fish should make the bottom flat. That way, the dish can serve as a tray or coaster for a couple of glasses and a bottle, or just a clutch of bottles.

The more traditional bowl shows how to get the most from an unpromising blank. You'll see the process whereby you establish the maximum amount of solid wood available from which to create the bowl and then how to turn the final form. Finally, there are two fragile pieces that are tricky to turn and that require special chucking techniques for completion.

Hollowing with Gouges

All hollowing cuts are made from a single direction. There is no need to use any type of cut other than a shear cut, moving from rim to center with the bevel rubbing the wood all the way. There should be little difference between the quality of the roughing cuts that remove the bulk of the waste and the final pass that fine-tunes the shape of the piece. Regard the early cuts as practice runs for the final ones that count the most.

A long bevel makes the gouge easier to start (**A**), but as the curve you're cutting swings toward the center, you'll need progressively steeper bevels to maintain bevel contact on different sections of a curve (**B**). I have three bowl gouges ready for use at any one time, each with a different bevel.

To begin roughing out, start the gouge on its side with the flute facing center. If you have problems with the tool kicking back, roll it clockwise a degree or two so the flute faces slightly downward. Hold the handle just below horizontal and keep the bevel aligned in the direction you want to cut (**C**). Keep your hand or finger planted firmly on the rest to prevent the tool from kicking back. To start the cut, raise the handle to pivot the edge through an arc into the wood.

Once the bevel is rubbing, rotate the tool slightly counterclockwise and drop the handle a few degrees for a fatter shaving (**D**). The bulk of the waste should curl off the right wing of the edge. Let the wood come to the tool, moving the tool forward ever slower as you approach center. Carry on around the curve as long as you can maintain bevel contact with the wood, aiming for a surface as clean as on this piece of elm (**E**). When bevel contact becomes impossible, change to a gouge with a steeper bevel. Or, near the base, you can also change to a heavy scraper (see photos C–E on p. 211).

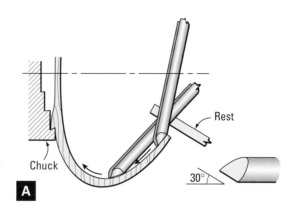

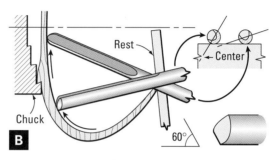

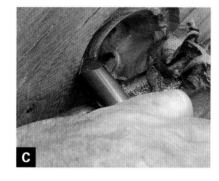

F

G

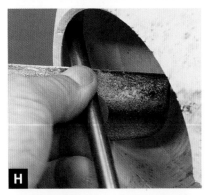

H

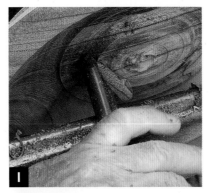

I

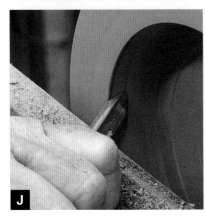

J

K

Enclosed forms are more of a challenge because, for the inside finishing cuts, the gouge handle starts on the other side of the lathe. Rather than lean over the bed, I move to the back of the lathe in order to cut under the rim **(F)**. Set the tool rest at right angles to the direction you're cutting, with the end projecting into the hollow **(A)**. Use a long-beveled ¼-in. (6mm) deep-fluted gouge for the entry cut **(G)**. Start the gouge on its side with the bevel aligned in the direction you're cutting. Once the gouge is in the wood with the bevel rubbing, rotate the tool slightly counterclockwise, taking care not to catch the left wing of the edge **(H)**. The small gouge will take you in about 1½ in. (40mm) before it starts to flex, after which you'll need to use a heavier gouge to finish the cut.

The bulk of the lower half of the waste can be removed with a long-beveled gouge on its side, sweeping into the center without the bevel rubbing **(I)**. Keep your hand firmly on the rest as a lateral fulcrum against which the tool pivots. This sweeping cut removes waste rapidly, but the ridged surface needs a smoothing cut with a steep beveled gouge or a scraper.

To cut straight in to a flat base, use a detail gouge with a long fingernail grind. Start the gouge on its side with the flute facing center, then roll it slightly counterclockwise for a better shaving **(J)**. At the end of the cut, roll the tool on its side so there's no danger of catching the left wing of the edge **(K)**.

▶ See *"Rough Hollowing with Scrapers"* on **facing page.**

Rough Hollowing with Scrapers

An advantage of roughing with scrapers is financial: scrapers are half the cost of bowl gouges. On abrasive timbers like teak, this can save grinding a lot of expensive gouge steel. For depths over 6 in. (150mm), scrapers are the only option, as standard gouges are rarely long enough to reach deeper, even when new. You can purchase bar steel for scrapers in almost any length and then, to make life really easy, use a deep-hollowing system that prevents the tool from grabbing.

When rough hollowing, use a ⅜-in.- (9mm-) thick square or round-nose scraper ¾ in. to 1 in. (19mm to 25mm) wide. Never cut with more than half the edge. Square-end scrapers should be pushed in as near parallel to the lathe axis as possible in a series of steps **(A)**, using less of the edge as you cut farther from the center. Never force the edge into the wood; if it doesn't cut easily, hone it sharp. If that's not enough to restore the edge, grind it. Round-nose scrapers should make sweeping cuts toward the chuck, taking the same path as a gouge **(B)**.

When hogging out waste at the bottom of a bowl, use a heavy scraper to sweep broadly to and from the center **(C)**, Use this technique only in the bottom half of a bowl. If you try this on a thin upper wall, the bowl will explode.

The final shaping of broad curves can be done with the same heavy, radiused scraper. Completing an internal curve in one sweep of a gouge is satisfying, but difficult. Across the bottom, I find it easier to use heavy scrapers, using the right side of the edge to develop the curve into the base in steps, easing the edge straight into the wood **(D, E)**.

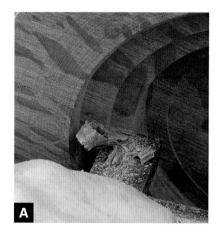

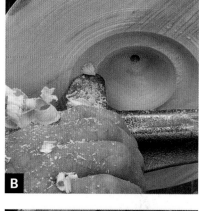

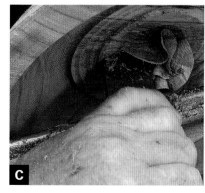

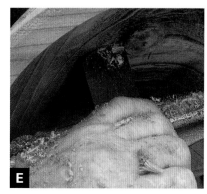

Finishing with Scrapers

Scrapers can be used to improve most gouge-cut surfaces, and they reign supreme on a flat-bottomed recess like that in a bottle coaster. That said, I never use a scraper flat on the rest anywhere near the rim of a bowl. If you have torn grain or chatter marks near a rim that resist removal with a gouge, shear scraping might do the job, but heavy sanding is a lot safer. Imprudent use of a scraper on thin wall—typically on the inside of a bowl rim—usually results in a terrifying catch that often splits the workpiece and ruins the job.

On the lower half of a curve, keep the scraper flat on the rest. The idea is to use only a small section of an edge that has a radius slightly tighter than the curve you are cutting **(A)**. (It's very difficult to cut smooth curves with a round-nose or domed scraper.) The point of cut drifts along the radiused edge as you move the tool along the rest. Use no more than ½ in. (13mm) of the edge at one time and make the cuts toward the center.

On a flat-bottomed recess, use a skewed scraper flat on the rest to get into a corner **(B)**. A gouge is the best tool for cutting a straight side cleanly, but it's worth trying a very sharp scraper corner **(C)**. Set the rest at center height so only the top left side of the tool blade contacts the wood; push the scraper forward very slowly while keeping it horizontal. If the handle wavers you won't get a smooth surface.

If you have to scrape near the rim of an out-flowing curve, you'll want to shear scrape, tilting a radiused edge on its side and cutting with only the lower half of the edge **(D)**. Keep your thumb on the rest against the tool blade to serve as a fulcrum. (Don't place your thumb on top of the tool where it's of no help.) Position your fingers at the back of the cut to equalize any tool pressure against the wood. Work very gently when making the cut.

To shear scrape an undercut rim, use an asymmetrical round-nose scraper on its side **(E)**, again supporting the back of the cut with your fingers while your thumb acts as fulcrum against the side of the blade.

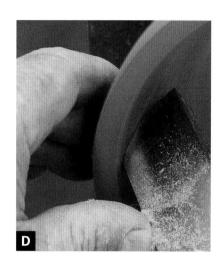

A

B

C

D

Nesting Bowls

As decent wood has become scarcer, interest in saving the center of bowls has revived. Before the days of power saws, pole-lathe turners often made nests of bowls in order to make best use of hard-won material. These days, we do it to maximize the yield from blanks of increasingly scarce and expensive material.

The technique involves turning the bowl profile, then using slicing tools for the nesting. Slicing is best done at low speeds, 300 rpm to 500 rpm.

> ⚠ **WARNING Never use high-speed steel (HSS) parting tools to nest bowls, as a heavy catch can snap the tools in two.**

The simplest method is to use a straight slicer, cutting in from the headstock side and aiming the cut at the center of the bowl base **(A)**. When a diameter of wood less than 3 in. (75mm) joins the bowl to the rest of the blank, the bowl starts vibrating. At this stage, you should be able to lever it free with a crowbar **(B, C)**. If the bowl blank won't break free, cut in a bit farther and try prying again.

Most bowl-nesting systems are designed to operate from the tailstock end of the lathe. The bowl profile is turned, then mounted in a chuck as for hollowing. Curved cutters slice out vaguely hemispherical bowls, starting with the smallest **(D)**. Shown is the popular McNaughton bowl saver, which can be ordered with left-side cutters for use when cutting from the headstock side. Peeling bowls off the blank from the headstock side is much faster, and the blank is held more securely.

Sushi Tray

Select a seasoned blank about 10 in. by 1½ in. (250mm by 40mm) and mount it on a faceplate or screw chuck. Turn the base slightly concave so the tray will sit on its rim. Then make a shallow groove about ⅛ in. (3mm) deep to accept the expanding jaws of your chuck, keeping as much mass as possible in the center of the base **(A)**. The wider the diameter of the recess—here 6¼ in. (160mm)—the more support you have for the workpiece when hollowing.

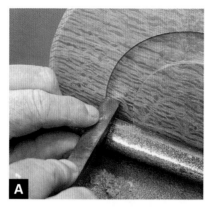

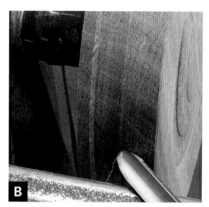

Next, turn the side using a gouge and scrapers to get the best surface before sanding **(B)**. Sand and finish the outside in preparation for turning the inside. Then remove the job from the chuck and use the drill press to drill a few depth holes **(C)**. Don't forget to allow for the depth of the chuck groove and aim to finish with the base ³⁄₁₆ in. (5mm) thick over the groove.

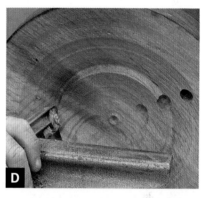

Mount the blank on the lathe, expanding the chuck within the groove. Remove the bulk of the interior with a bowl gouge, stopping to check the depth of your cut against the depth of the drilled holes **(D)**. Use a square-end scraper to obtain a flat bottom, checking your progress with a small straightedge. For these tight situations, I use a shopmade triangle of scrap medium-density fiberboard (MDF) **(E)**. To prevent chatter marks, you'll need a very delicate touch when turning across the bottom. If you press too hard, the high pitch of the cut will attack your eardrums.

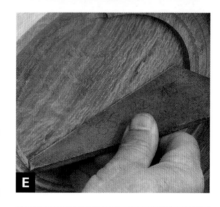

When the bottom is done, use the nose of a detail gouge on its side to shear cut the vertical wall **(F)**. Then you'll need a scraper again to clean up the bottom corner, after which you'll be ready to sand and finish the tray **(G)**.

A

B

C

D

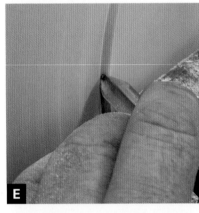
E

F

G

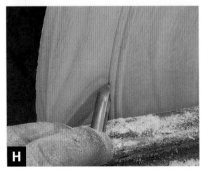
H

Bowl

The approach on any blank is to cut away anything you don't want in the finished object as early as possible. This means removing all splits, rot, and bark, although it's tempting to retain the latter if it seems firmly attached. However, bark is inevitably subject to insect attack, like sapwood, and it might also eventually separate. Therefore, it is good practice to remove all bark to guard against that possibility. I usually get rid of the sapwood as well.

This 16-in.- (400mm-) diameter blank was cut to ensure a rim of solid wood above the bark (see photos G and H on p. 63). Then it was fixed to a screw chuck on the lathe. On a blank like this, with its bark inclusions, mark the upper and lower limits of the bark as well as a possible diameter for the base (**A**). Then use a gouge to turn away the bark between the lines (**B**). As the bark reduces, it helps to re-mark its borders (**C**) so you don't remove more than you have to as you cut back to solid wood.

At this stage, a diameter for the foot is laid out (**D**). Here, it is sized to fit into a 5⅛-in. (130mm) step jaw. After the waste is removed on the base, turn the foot about ³⁄₁₆ in. (5mm) high using a ⅜-in. (9mm) detail gouge (**E**).

Complete the shaping of the profile using a gouge (**F**) and a scraper to refine the surface, particularly around the roughed beads (**G**). Then shape the beads with a detail gouge (**H**).

Sand and finish the whole of the outside in preparation for remounting in the step jaws **(I)**.

Rough out the bulk of the inside with a bowl gouge **(J)**, using your fingers to deflect the shavings downward **(K)**. While the bowl wall is still thick, cut the rim. Position your thumb on the rest and against the side of the gouge, with your fingers supporting the rim behind the point of cut **(L)**. Then cut the curve in from the rim toward the base **(M)**, moving the tool forward slowly to leave as smooth a surface as possible **(N)**.

At this stage, you can transfer to a gouge with a steeper bevel, but I prefer to use a heavy scraper to cut a series of steps toward the center as I extend the curve from the rim **(O, P)**.

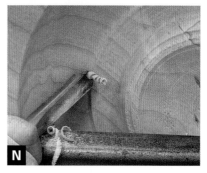

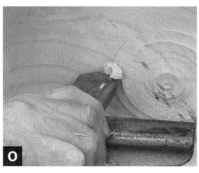

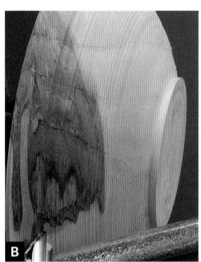

Truing Roughed Bowls

It is common practice to rough turn bowls to hasten seasoning. Rough-hollowed bowls need a wall thickness at least 15 percent the diameter of the bowl, unless the wood is renowned for its stability **(A)**. When rough turning, you'll need to shape a foot to fit your chuck for remounting the bowl for completion after seasoning. A typical roughed-bowl profile is shown in **(B)**. Ensure that the bottom is flat or slightly concave so it is easier to locate in the chuck when you come to remount it.

► See *"Nesting Bowls"* on p. 214.

If you rough turn using a faceplate instead of a chuck, fix the bowl to the faceplate using two screws aligned along the grain. That way, you can use the same holes later for completing the seasoned blank. If you orient the screws across the grain, they will move closer together as the wood shrinks in its width. Before chucks were available, I employed this method using two #14 wood screws penetrating the wood no more than $\frac{7}{16}$ in. (11mm). On bowls less than 8 in. (200mm) in diameter, I reduced the effective length of the screws by using washers to lessen the possibility of hitting the screws when hollowing the bowl. Ultimately, the screw holes need plugging. You could turn the holes away instead, but that's a fearful waste of good material.

Once a bowl is seasoned, remount it as accurately as you can with the foot in the chuck. I say "as accurately as you can" because the bowl (and its foot) will have warped to an oval shape in the seasoning process. After the bowl is mounted, use a square-end scraper to turn a shoulder in the interior **(C)** against which to expand the chuck jaws for the next step of truing the profile and foot.

Next, reverse the bowl onto the expanding jaws **(D)**. Now that the bowl is held securely, turn the profile true **(E)** and remove any undesirable splits or defects that developed during seasoning. The profile you'll be able turn will now depend on how much of the original roughed bowl is remaining and the thickness of its thinnest sections. If the roughed bowl warped considerably, use calipers to check the wall thickness in the thin sections. Mark the location of thin areas on the bowl profile, using a pencil, as when defining bark (see C on p. 216). As you turn the final shape, the lines will indicate areas that cannot be turned any thinner.

If you want to true a roughed bowl using a faceplate instead of a chuck, begin by planing or sanding the base flat. Mount the faceplate to the bowl bottom with screws, then complete the bowl in one fixing, plugging the screw holes afterward.

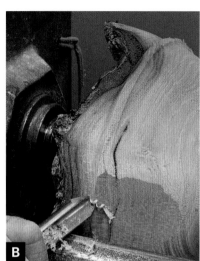

Natural-Edge Bowl

This mulberry bowl was turned from the blank shown in photos F–I on p. 77. The intention here is to orient the highest points on the rim of the finished bowl in the same horizontal plane and the two smaller spikes in between on their own horizontal plane. The blank is mounted between centers so it can be manipulated to bring the points into the desired alignment.

The key to turning a natural-edged bowl (or any bowl with an undulating edge) is to move the tool smoothly as it intermittently contacts wood in the gapped areas. There must be minimal tool pressure against the wood, otherwise the tool may slip into the gap and shatter the bowl as the rim slams down against it. This bowl begins with the bark apparently less than secure in places. To prevent losing these sections, I flooded the bark with thin cyanoacrylate (CA) adhesive and filled any gaps with thicker, gap-filling CA glue. Unfortunately, a section broke free anyway. As a result, I ultimately picked off the remainder of the bark because I believe that no bark looks better than only some bark.

Initial cuts with a gouge remove all the flat facets from the base up to the bark **(A)**. After that, the section with the bark is trued, cutting in from the top **(B)**. With a bowl mounted between centers, complete all the profile you can reach. In the process, turn a temporary foot to fit your chuck for the next mounting. In this case, mulberry finishes well with a scraper flat on the rest **(C)**. However, where there is bark and space, it is infinitely safer to tilt the scraper on edge to shear scrape **(D)**. A shear scraper is unlikely to catch if you cut with the lower half of the edge. When the outside is turned, remount the bowl for hollowing.

In preparation for drilling the depth hole, begin by cutting through the bark to solid wood at the center. Then set the rest square to the lathe bed and measure the depth required from the rest—here marked with masking tape on the drill **(E)**. Drill the hole using the rest as a guide **(F)**.

First hollow to center, retaining a wall thick enough to resist flexing **(G)**. On this 6¾-in.- (175mm-) diameter bowl a ¾-in. (19mm) wall is sufficient. On larger bowls, a 1-in.- (25mm-) thick wall should be enough. The final cuts in from the rim should travel into solid wood just below the bark line. Regard your first rim cuts as a practice for the final cuts **(H)**. I make the rim cut using a ⅜-in. (9mm) bowl gouge, then transfer to the heavier ½-in. (13mm) bowl gouge for the cut into center. Any ridges or chatter marks can be removed by shear scraping **(I)**.

[TIP] **Don't even think about using a scraper flat on the rest near any rim, let alone one as fragile as this.**

Extend the curve into the bottom using a heavy radiused scraper in broad sweeping passes. Sand everything you can get at. Power sanding is the safest and most controlled way to smooth the rim sections.

➤ See *"Power Sanding"* on p. 235.

E

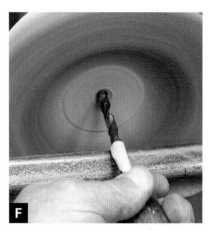

F

G

H

I

J

K

L

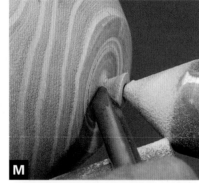

M

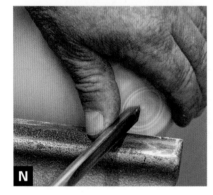

N

O

To remove the foot or refine the base of an uneven rimmed bowl, place it over a rounded disc covered with cloth and locate the tail center in its original position **(J)**. Remove the waste with small peeling cuts. A small detail gouge is handiest for this job **(K)**. Then blend the new and old surfaces by shear scraping **(L)**. Any slight eccentricity will vanish during sanding.

Finally, use a long-beveled detail gouge to cut into the center **(M)**. Chances are the last tiny bit will cleave, leaving the small cone of wood static on the center while still supporting the workpiece. Often, the bowl is secure enough over the chuck to be finished off without tail-center support **(N)**. However, it is essential that you keep your hand against the bowl all the time to ensure it doesn't drop off. Prepare yourself by making sure that any abrasives or tools you might need are within easy reach **(O)**.

Enclosed Form

This rounded form is an enclosed variation of the natural-edge bowl but is turned from a square blank. The blank is driven by a faceplate spur drive (see photos F–I on p. 77). As usual, initial cuts with a gouge remove waste from the corner to reduce the weight as quickly as possible **(A)**. The split at the bottom will ultimately need to be removed, but for now it can be retained within a rechucking foot.

Begin to shape the top, cutting from the chuck back to the fullness of the curve **(B)**. Then refine the profile as far as you can, using the gouge and a skewed scraper, projecting the upper part of the curve toward the center and inward of the drive spurs **(C)**.

Remount the job in a chuck for hollowing, keeping the tailstock in place for extra support while you finalize the curve into the rim **(D)**. The hole for hollowing is both small and fragile, and the bark is likely to break off with the slightest pressure. After drilling the depth hole, take out the bulk with scrapers. If necessary, stand at the far side of the lathe so you can get your weight over the tool handle **(E)**. Here, I was able to just get in with a very long-beveled ¼-in. (6mm) gouge **(F)**. I cut most of the bark cleanly, but then the gouge proved too whippy, so I went back to scrapers to complete the inside. After the inside is hollowed, sand everything you can reach.

To complete the base, mount the form into the hole of a jam chuck **(G)**. Here, I used a failed bowl for the chuck. Use the tail center to keep the workpiece in the chuck as you remove the waste and to shape the base, proceeding as shown in K–N opposite.

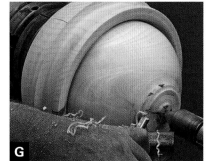

Sanding and Finishing, page 226

PART SIX

Sanding and Finishing

IN RECENT YEARS an enormous number of products for sanding and finishing turned objects have been developed. Today, a host of commercial products developed for industry are also manufactured for the huge amateur woodworking market. New abrasives make for faster and more efficient sanding, as do new techniques and tools for using them. Any surface can be smoothed in a few minutes.

Once sanded, turned wood is usually sealed with a finish to protect it from dirty fingers and accidental stains as well as the changes in humidity that can warp most timbers. The array of waxes and oils for finishing is bewildering, although most are variations of each other. Some take seconds or minutes to apply, others take hours or even days.

The degree to which you sand a particular object and the finish you choose to put on it will depend partly on that object's function and partly on your preference for a matte or gloss luster.

Sanding and Finishing

Preparation

➤ Repairing Knots and Splits (p. 233)

Basic Sanding

➤ Hand-Sanding Face Work (p. 234)

➤ Power Sanding (p. 235)

➤ Sanding a Cove (p. 236)

➤ Sanding Spindles (p. 237)

➤ Final Preparation for Finishing (p. 238)

Advanced Sanding

➤ Sanding a Natural Edge (p. 239)

➤ Deep Holes and Small Openings (p. 240)

Finishes

➤ Applying a Finish (p. 241)

THE PURPOSE OF A FINISH is to protect wood against stains, grubby fingers, spilled wine, rings left by hot mugs, and the variations in humidity that can cause swelling and shrinkage. But a finish is also aesthetic, lending a piece much of its character and style. Most people love the glowing, slippery-smooth surface on well-used, much-handled wooden objects. Unfortunately, this isn't available in bottles. It's called a patina, and it is the result of years of care, handling, and exposure to air and light.

A patina happens naturally, but you can help it along. The old rule of thumb for developing a patina on wood is to polish it every day for a month, then every week for a year, then every month thereafter. However, years of constant interaction with soft, sweaty hands is a better alternative. The best thing we can do for wood is to lay the foundations for that patina to happen, then encourage keepers of our work to take ongoing care of the object.

Of course, the type of object helps determine the appropriate finish. A box intended for rings or pills needs a different

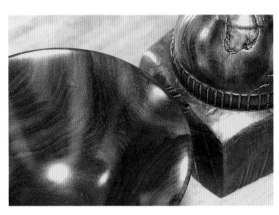

Regular polishing over several years creates a deep patina.

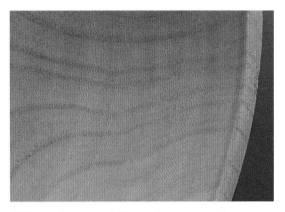

This surface could have been cut cleaner, but sanding soon removed the gouge marks on this 10-in. (250mm) ash bowl.

finish (at least internally) than a box made to contain curry paste. Bread or chopping boards do not require the fine sanding or high polish that brings out chatoyance on African blackwood. And a rustic chair might lose much of its presence if its cleanly cut spindles are sanded. So you need to decide two things: What degree of surface preparation is required for the job and then which finish is most appropriate.

Surface Preparation

Any finish you apply will highlight defects or sanding marks, so surface preparation is of vital importance. The handles I make for my tools are left unsanded because I get a little hit of smug satisfaction every time I pick one up—congratulating myself that the handle was so nicely turned that it didn't need sanding. For items subject to considerable wear and tear, like chopping boards, sanding to 150 grit should create a fine enough surface. On architectural spindles that will be painted, 120 grit is better because paint cannot key onto very smooth surfaces.

During the 1970s, as I developed my reputation as a turner, I rarely sanded finer than 180 grit on anything. That was the norm then. Now I go to 320 grit on most woods, and to 600 grit on dense hardwoods. Still, that is not as fine as seems common practice these days among studio turners. For a while, I sanded everything to 600 grit, but found that people wouldn't use such smooth bowls for fear of ruining the surface. I see no point in creating utilitarian objects that people won't use, hence my current sanding practice.

Although sanding can remove a lot of tool marks, it's always preferable to turn the wood as cleanly as possible to begin with.

Sanding

Abrasives for sanding are commercially available in sheets and rolls that are torn into manageable pieces for use. Abrasive discs are also available to fit on pads for power sanding. All abrasives are graded by number, with higher numbers indicating finer grits. To obtain a scratch-free surface, work through a range of successively finer grits to the smoothness you desire, moving up to a finer grit only when no outstanding scratches from the previous grit remain. I typically begin with 100 grit, work my way through 150 and 220, then finish up with 320 grit. However, I occasionally start with 60 grit when I fail to cut the wood cleanly enough. And occasionally I'll finish with 600 grit.

Abrasives need to be flexible to avoid scoring rounded hollows. Best are those backed with light cloth or foam. I generally avoid paper-backed abrasives as they become either damp and floppy in humid conditions or so crisp in dry conditions that they crack or split when folded, creating sharp corners. Abrasives are easiest to use in hand-size sheets folded in three, so one portion of grit never rubs against another.

When sanding face work by hand on the lathe, keep the abrasive in the lower left quadrant (as you face the headstock), either pulled away from the center or pressed toward the headstock. Reduce the strain on your right arm by pulling it with your left hand. This also provides better control and leverage. And whenever possible, use the rest

Keep the abrasive in the lower left quadrant pressed either away from the center or toward the headstock.

and headstock for extra support and control. Bend the leading edge of the sheet away from the oncoming wood so it doesn't catch.

Careless sanding can cost detail. Concentrate on one surface at a time so you don't inadvertently round over edges and lose turned detail. For example, when sanding the hollowed interior of a bowl, at first pay no attention to the rim. Then sand the rim with no hint of attention to the interior. Having said that, the edges of a rim can become slicing sharp, so develop the habit of dabbing them occasionally with the abrasive you're using to remove the razor edge, taking care not to round them over.

Heat generated from the friction of sanding can crack the wood, so it helps to drop the speed slightly from your turning speed. On a variable-speed lathe, a 200 rpm to 300 rpm decrease will do; on a lathe with pulleys only, it's okay to maintain the turning speed if adjusting the belts is awkward.

Abrasives are easiest to use in hand-size sheets folded in three, so one portion of grit never rubs against another portion.

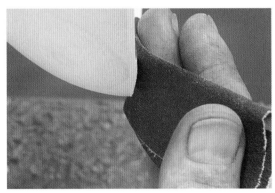

Be positive about sanding one surface then another, in order not to lose the turned detail.

> **SANDING AND FINISHING SAFELY**

Sanding is a monotonous activity that can lead to a wandering mind. However, you need to concentrate, as it is easy to ruin the form you turned by inadvertently rounding over edges or letting bumps and dips develop. To prevent hurting yourself or your work, follow these three basic safety rules:

- Never stick your fingers in small holes with the lathe running. This can lead to some nasty, bloodless, cauterized-as-you-go cuts on your fingers. Use a sanding stick instead.

- Beware of sharp edges. If you're not careful, razor-sharp edges can develop in seconds on rims, particularly on end-grain projects like goblets. Develop the habit of softening all edges regularly during the sanding process.

- Never wrap abrasives or rags around your fingers. If the other end is caught by the spinning workpiece, you'll find yourself in a quick bind and could lose a finger.

If the work does crack from the heat caused by sanding too long and hard, let the wood cool, then sand using fine abrasives with the lathe switched off until you can't *feel* the splits. Chances are you'll be able to see them, but there's little you can do about that. Fortunately, as the wood inevitably darkens with age, the cracks will become less noticeable.

[TIP] **Sanding is a dusty business, so collect the dust at the source, and sand so the dust is flung in the direction of the dust-collection hood.**

Types of Finish

There are hundreds of commercially available finishes based on oils and waxes, lacquers, urethanes, melamine, and cellulose, each seemingly with slightly different methods of application. The finishes come in jars and bottles as creams and liquids or as wrapped lumps.

Finishes are divided broadly into those that penetrate the wood and those that sit on the surface. The penetrating oil finishes harden inside the wood to provide an excellent base for a patina that will improve with age, whereas surface finishes tend to break up and deteriorate after a few years.

Finishes generally give the wood either a soft sheen, like that at the left, or a gloss

Left: These trays were made around 1973 and used daily since. Although the tray at the left was treated with a well-known brand of finish guaranteed to repel acids, water, and heat, the finish began to disintegrate after 5 years of use. The other two trays were originally oiled and waxed. *Right:* The refurbished tray has been oiled, the others have been washed, and the one at the front right has been oiled very occasionally.

Finishes generally give the wood either a soft sheen (*left*) or a gloss (*right*).

finish, as shown to the right, in the photo at left. The finish applied to the left is a U-Beaut Polishes traditional wax, with the same company's Shellawax finish seen on the right side.

A tough, shiny surface built up from layers of lacquer, shellac, or two-part epoxy might look great at point of sale in a gallery or on vases sitting untouched in a display cabinet. In the long run, however, even the hardest and most durable finishes will chip, crack, flake, or simply wear away, sometimes in as few as 10 years—as I've witnessed on several turnings I've collected. Water is also a danger. When water blotches a finish, a deterioration begins that eventually deprives the object of its appeal. With the difficulty of repairing some finishes, it is no wonder that flea markets are full of wooden objects with damaged finishes.

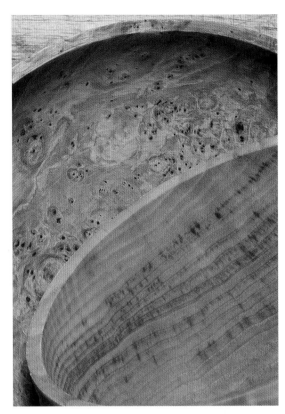

Bowls in daily use are washed but not oiled. Abraded daily by lettuce, these have become ultra-smooth.

Selecting a Finish

There is no one "perfect" surface or finish, so you need to have some concept of how a completed object will be used. How do you see it aging, and under what circumstances? Will a bowl be used or will it sit on a shelf as a decorative object? If it's to be used, what will it be used for? Letters? Keys? Salad? Farm-fresh eggs? Fruit? And what will happen to the finish in hot water?

When you choose a finish, know what you want to achieve, apart from bringing out the grain and beauty of the timber. The finish you use should depend on the nature of the object as well as your personal preference for a low-sheen, gloss, or high-gloss surface.

Do you aspire to your work lasting decades or generations as I do? Or are you content with a finish that will last just a few years at most.

I finish my utilitarian bowls, boxes, platters, and scoops with a simple mixture of oil and beeswax, which provides a good base for regular polishing. It also looks fine on a retailer's shelf. More important, it comes off with hot water and detergent, so food bowls used daily can be washed along with the regular dishes (but not in a dishwasher). Like kitchen chopping boards, salad bowls and wooden plates in constant use need no ongoing oiling. The food bowls I use day to day (at left) have, over the years, each developed a soft matte character and have become ultra-smooth. You can't beat lettuce or oatmeal as a fine abrasive. Each bowl is washed in hot water and detergent, but never oiled.

If you are finishing bowls, spoons, scoops, platters, boards, or anything else likely to be used for food, you need a nontoxic finish. For food-related items, walnut oil is the traditional food-safe finish in France, and it is becoming increasingly popular elsewhere. Another long-established food-safe finish is tung oil, which penetrates well into wood, then dries to a hard, transparent matte finish. In addition to these, there are many salad bowl and chopping board finishes commercially available through specialist woodturning stores and catalogs.

Through three decades of turning wood, I've tried many commercial finishes, including a variety of waxes. I decided against using carnauba wax early in my career when I realized how tricky it is to apply evenly, and how difficult it is to repair when spotted with water. Most of the softer paste waxes

Polishing with oil or wax transforms a sanded surface. Here the center is raw wood, ringed by an oil and beeswax finish.

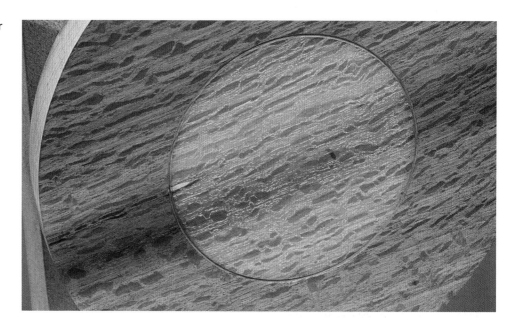

that produce the finish I prefer seem to consist of little more than the boiled linseed oil and the beeswax that I use now or the paraffin wax I've used in the past. Many oil and wax finishes can be applied in less than a minute to work that's mounted on the lathe. This is great for production and fine for food bowls, but it does require occasional maintenance from its owner. So, since 1970, I have put the following label on all my utilitarian bowls: "Richard Raffan made this bowl to be used. Hand wash in hot water and detergent, and wipe with vegetable oil occasionally. Cared for, it will look better for use and should survive us all."

Better is an oil-based finish that penetrates the wood, then hardens within it, providing a foundation onto which you can build layers of wax to create the sort of high shine found on antique furniture.

Applying Finishes

Many finishes are potentially dangerous during application, so heed the warnings on the packaging. Those containing solvents are not good for your lungs, and I've avoided them for that reason. Solvents are also a fire hazard and should be kept well clear of the grinder and its sparks. You need to be careful with rags used for some oils like the boiled linseed I use. Crumpled up rags can ignite spontaneously, so spread used rags out to dry. Trash them only after they are stiff.

Most turnings are easily finished on a lathe by applying shellac, oil, or wax to the spinning wood using a soft cloth and running the lathe slowly to prevent splattering oil everywhere. This transforms a dull sanded surface, like that at the center of the disc in the photo above to one with bright color, like at the perimeter. Polishing wood on a lathe is one of those activities that, once experienced, you'll continue to anticipate with relish.

Repairing Knots and Splits

Often, small knots, splits, and slits can prove to be irritations on an otherwise satisfactory surface. These are best packed with fine dust set in place with adhesive. Contrasting dark dust or powder-paint generally looks most natural. The best filler I've found is the powder I get when boring into the end grain of African blackwood box blanks with a scraper or drill. However, black powder paint also works well.

Work the dust into the split with your fingers **(A)**, then drip on enough cyanoacrylate glue to flood through the dust **(B)**. A few drops will do it. Use accelerator spray to set the glue if necessary (although many dense tropical hardwoods harden the resin faster than the accelerator). Any surface mess is soon sanded away **(C)**.

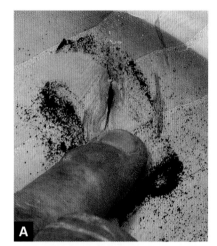

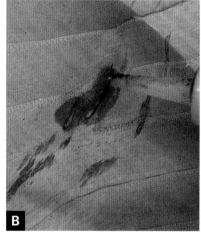

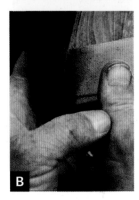

Hand-Sanding Face Work

To hand-sand a flat surface, use abrasive wrapped around a rectangular scrap of medium density fiberboard (MDF) **(A)**. Keep the block moving between the rim and just across center to ensure a flat face. If a dome develops at the center, stop the lathe and rotate the job with your left hand while sanding across the center with your right.

On thin-walled outflowing bowls, equalize sanding pressure with your hand on the other side of the bowl wall **(B)**. Otherwise, you risk the whole bowl shattering under excess pressure. Enclosed forms are much stronger, but ensure that the leading edge of the abrasive is curled clear of the wood, especially on an uneven rim **(C)**.

Power Sanding

Face work is most efficiently sanded using a disc on a foam-backed pad mounted in a drill. On larger projects, power sanding reduces sanding time considerably, while on the inside of a small bowl, power sanding is a handy technique for first refining your curve, then maintaining it across the center.

Angle drills (we're not talking higher-speed angle grinders) are far easier to use than conventional drills. Although more expensive than conventional drills, angle drills can be controlled using just one hand, freeing up the other to support delicate jobs **(A)**. Conventional drills tend to kick about if not securely gripped with both hands, and you'll need to lock the drive spindle to secure the job **(B)**. If you intend to make a lot of bowls or vases, an angle drill is a great tool to have in your kit.

You can safely power sand anywhere in the bottom third of a bowl using the sander so it rotates against the oncoming wood **(C)**.

A rotary sander, with its freewheeling sanding pad, works like a small motorless angle drill **(D)**. The pad rotates when pressed against the spinning wood, leaving few (if any) swirl marks. It is an excellent finishing tool, although not as effective as a drill-mounted pad for heavy sanding across center.

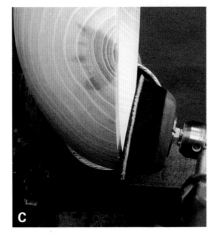

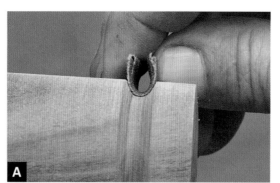

A

B

C

Sanding a Cove

On a cove, don't let the abrasive ooze over the edges and round the rims. Pinch the sheet into a U-shape **(A)**, or wrap it around a dowel or oval pencil **(B)**. After you're done with the groove, sand the adjacent surfaces **(C)**.

Sanding Spindles

To sand a spindle, wrap a folded sheet around it, pinching the abrasive against the surface **(A)**. Thin spindles need extra support, especially when mounted in a chuck without a tail center. Whenever possible, use the rest or headstock to steady your hand **(B, C)**.

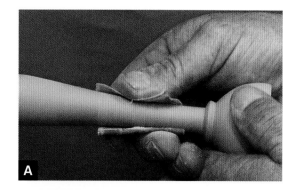

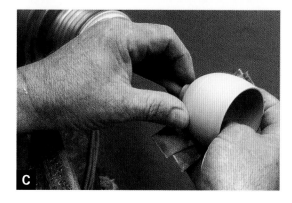

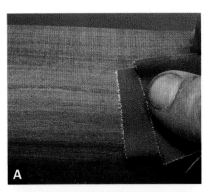

A

Final Preparation for Finishing

Applying a finish usually highlights any defects in a sanded surface. Fine scratch marks or rings from sanding can really mar an object, but they are easy to eliminate if you sand with the grain. Stop the lathe and sand back and forth along the grain to remove all cross-grain scratches **(A)**.

Dust is a real enemy of most finishes. Unfortunately, dust from sanding can get trapped in burl fissures **(B)**. This must be removed before finishing. You can get most of it out with a brush, but there's nothing like compressed air to get rid of it entirely.

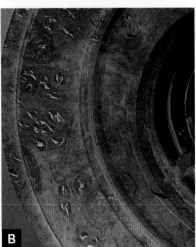

B

Sanding a Natural Edge

If you sand natural edges with the lathe running, the leading edge of each peak will be sanded thinner than the trailing edge, which looks terrible. Sanding natural edges is best done with a power sander and with the lathe switched off. Done correctly, this will result in peaks of consistent thickness. To sand a profile, hold the drill steady against your side while rotating the job back and forth by hand against the sander **(A)**, keeping a close eye on the wall thickness. To sand the interior, lock the lathe spindle so the section you're sanding is at about five o'clock, then move the sander across the static wood **(B)**. Use the same technique for any areas of difficult grain.

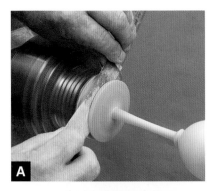

A

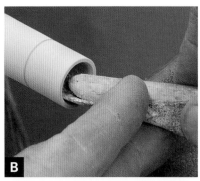

B

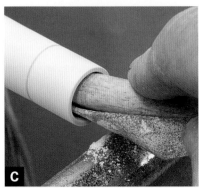

C

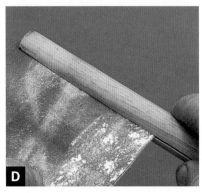

D

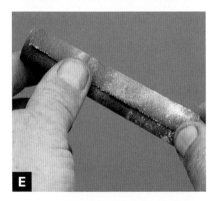

E

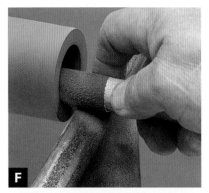

F

G

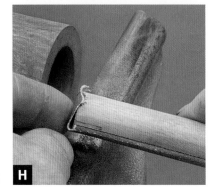

H

Deep Holes and Small Openings

Whenever an opening is too small to provide finger access, insert the abrasive using a sanding stick or flexible ruler. To sand the faces of a parting cut, wrap abrasive around a rule and bend it slightly to put pressure against the face you're sanding **(A)**.

In very small openings, like the interior of this salt scoop, fold a narrow strip of abrasive and prod it in with a bit of dowel rounded over to match the inner profile **(B, C)**.

On deeper hollows and internal cylinders, wrap abrasive around a slotted dowel. Insert the right-hand edge into the slot and wrap it around the stick **(D, E)**. Keep your finger on the back to prevent the sheet from unraveling as you move it against the wood. On deep hollows, use the tool rest to control the leverage **(F, G)**. To sand the flat bottom of a deep hole in end grain, bend the abrasive over the end of the stick **(H)**.

Applying a Finish

For most finishes the application process is much the same. With the lathe off, wipe the liquid finish or paste into the wood with a soft cloth **(A)**. When applying oil, continue as long as the wood wants to suck it up. You'll find that some woods absorb like a sponge, so keep applying the oil until it remains on the surface. Then wipe away the surplus **(B)** and run the lathe at sanding speed or slightly faster. Buff the surface hard and evenly with the same cloth to generate some heat **(C)**. This will open the wood pores and allow the oil to move farther into the wood. The process should leave the surface slightly oily.

Next apply a layer of wax to the surface. When using a block or stick of wax, hold it firmly against the spinning wood. This will generate friction and heat that melts the wax. **(D)**. Drag the block from center to rim. This deposits a thick layer of wax, which you next melt into the wood by moving a soft cloth firmly across the surface. On thin walls, support the backside of the surface with your left hand. Finally, with the lathe still running, use a clean cloth or paper towel to wipe the surface dry **(E)**.

When finishing burls and other fissured surfaces, I finish jobs off the lathe. After blasting away any impacted dust with compressed air, I swamp the wood with boiled linseed oil and set it aside for 15 hours to 18 hours to drain. Then before the oil dries, the job goes back on the lathe to spin out any surplus oil. Next, I buff the surface with a lint-free cotton rag that won't disintegrate or be torn by the fissures in the wood. Very fragile objects like scoops and ladles are finished in the same manner, but hand wiped and buffed off the lathe. It is important to wipe away surplus oil before it pools and hardens, because buffing it away afterward is tedious.

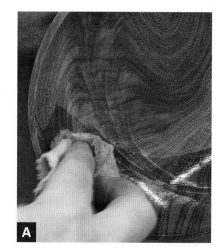

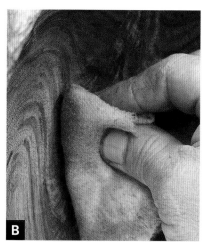

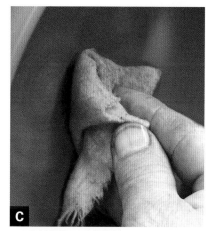

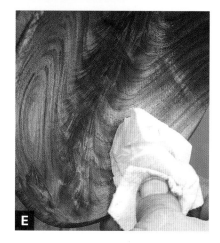

Further Reading

SETTING UP

Bird, Lonnie. *The Bandsaw Book.* The Taunton Press, 1999.

Nagyszalanczy, Sandor. *Woodshop Dust Control.* The Taunton Press, 1996.

SHARPENING

Lee, Leonard. *The Complete Guide to Sharpening.* The Taunton Press, 1995.

WOOD

Alexander, John. *Making a Chair from a Tree.* Taunton Press, 1978.

O'Donnell, Michael. *Turning Green Wood.* Guild of Master Craftsmen, 2000.

Hoadley, Bruce. *Understanding Wood.* The Taunton Press, 1980.

Malloff, Will. *Chainsaw Lumbermaking.* The Taunton Press, 1982.

WOODTURNING TECHNIQUE

Mortimer, Stuart. *Techniques of Spiral Work.* Lyons and Burford, 1995.

Raffan, Richard. *Turning Wood with Richard Raffan.* The Taunton Press, 2001.

Raffan, Richard. *Turning Bowls with Richard Raffan.* The Taunton Press, 2002.

Raffan, Richard. *Turning Boxes with Richard Raffan.* The Taunton Press, 2002.

THREAD CHASING

Darlow, Mike. *Woodturning Techniques.* Fox Chapel, 2001.

Holtzapffel, John Jacob. *Hand or Simple Turning.* Dover Publications, 1990.

FINISHES

Dresdner, Michael. *The New Wood Finishing Book.* The Taunton Press, 1999.

The Editors of *Fine Woodworking. Finishes and Finishing Techniques.* The Taunton Press, 1999.

Index

Other Books in the Series:

HARDCOVER

The Complete Illustrated Guide to Joinery
Gary Rogowski
ISBN 1-56158-401-0
Product #070535
$39.95

The Complete Illustrated Guide to Furniture and Cabinet Construction
Andy Rae
ISBN 1-56158-402-9
Product #070534
$39.95

The Complete Illustrated Guide to Shaping Wood
Lonnie Bird
ISBN 1-56158-400-2
Product #070533
$39.95

Taunton's Complete Illustrated Guide to Finishing
Jeff Jewitt
ISBN 1-56158-592-0
Product #070712
$39.95

Taunton's Complete Illustrated Guide to Sharpening
Tom Lie-Nielson
ISBN 1-56158-657-9
Product #70737
$42.00

Taunton's Complete Illustrated Guide to Using Woodworking Tools
Lonnie Bird
ISBN 1-56158-597-1
Product #70729
$42.00

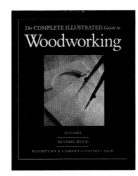

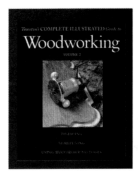

THE COMPLETE ILLUSTRATED GUIDES SLIPCASE SET

The Complete Illustrated Guide to Joinery

The Complete Illustrated Guide to Furniture and Cabinet Construction

The Complete Illustrated Guide to Shaping Wood
ISBN 1-56158-602-1
Product #070665
$120.00

THE COMPLETE ILLUSTRATED GUIDES SLIPCASE SET

Taunton's Complete Illustrated Guide to Using Woodworking Tools

Taunton's Complete Illustrated Guide to Sharpening

Taunton's Complete Illustrated Guide to Finishing
ISBN 1-56158-745-1
Product #070817
$126.00

PAPERBACK

Taunton's Complete Illustrated Guide to Period Furniture Details
Lonnie Bird
ISBN 1-56158-590-4
Product #070708
$27.00

Taunton's Complete Illustrated Guide to Choosing and Installing Hardware
Bob Setttich
ISBN 1-56158-561-0
Product #070647
$29.95

Taunton's Complete Illustrated Guide to Box Making
Doug Stowe
ISBN 1-56158-593-9
Product #070721
$24.95